Water and Poverty
in the Southwest

WATER AND POVERTY IN THE SOUTHWEST

F. LEE BROWN AND HELEN M. INGRAM

with contributions from Gilbert Bonem,
Wade Martin, Thomas R. McGuire,
Stephen F. Mumme, Luis Torres,
Mary Wallace, and Gary Weatherford

The University of Arizona Press

TUCSON

Publication of this book was assisted
by a grant from the Ford Foundation,
which also facilitated research by grants
to the John Muir Institute of Napa,
California, with which the authors
are affiliated.

THE UNIVERSITY OF ARIZONA PRESS

This book was set in 9½/12½ ITC Bookman Light.
Manufactured in the U.S.A.

Library of Congress Cataloging-in-Publication Data

Brown, F. Lee (Franklin Lee)
    Water and poverty in the southwest.

    Bibliography: p.
    Includes index.
    1. Water-supply, Rural—Southwestern States.
2. Rural poor—Southwestern States. I. Ingram,
Helen M., 1937–   . II. Bonem, Gilbert W.
III. Title.
HD1695.A165B76   1987   333.91'00979   87-19217
ISBN 0-8165-1038-5 (alk. paper)
ISBN 0-8165-1047-4 (pbk. : alk. paper)

British Library Cataloguing in Publication data are available.

To Ann and David

whose patient support and
encouragement helped us through
the difficult moments

CONTENTS

MAPS

TABLES

ACKNOWLEDGMENTS

This book is the cumulative result of a number of years of thought, discussion, observation, and participation in the water affairs of the American West. As such, it owes a considerable debt to numerous individuals with whom water issues have been discussed and debated throughout these years. However, there are individuals to whom we are especially appreciative. First and foremost are the contributors, particularly Gary and Gil, who worked with us and without whom the book would not have been possible. Their names are listed on the title page. In addition to them, Tim De Young, Charles DuMars, Bernard Fontana, Allen Kneese, Dean Mann, Maria Varela, and Nat Wollman provided critical but very helpful scrutiny of the manuscripts at various stages in its development, as did the unnamed reviewers selected by the University of Arizona Press. Research assistance was provided by Denis Antolini, Maureen Burdetti, Ann Jones, Ramona Peters, Karen Tsao, and Catherine Vandemoer.

Support of a different sort came from many others. The research that underlies the book was made possible by grants from the Ford Foundation, and we are particularly indebted to Norm Collins, Susan Sechler, and Jim Butcher in that regard. Administrative assistance was provided by Max Linn, Taylor Miller, Julie Hillis, and Angela Dolan of the John Muir Institute, and especially by Robin Morgan of the Natural Resources Center at the University of New Mexico and Kari Askey of the University of Arizona.

Finally but most fundamentally, we are indebted to the numerous Hispanic citizens of the Upper Rio Grande communities in northern New Mexico and southern Colorado and to the many Tohono O'odham tribal members of southern Arizona who shared with us their thoughts and feelings concerning their precious water resource. We hope our words may be as helpful to them as theirs were to us.

F. LEE BROWN AND HELEN M. INGRAM

Water and Poverty
in the Southwest

Counties of the Southwest containing
a substantial degree of poverty.

CHAPTER 1

Water and the Rural Poor
in the Southwest: An Overview

Water Runs from the Poor and Powerless

"Water flows uphill to money" is a popular adage in the arid Southwest.[1] It succinctly captures the well-understood economic and political reality that water is, indeed, controlled by wealth and power. Fradkin has remarked, "When it comes to distributing water in the West, it has been the politically strong and aggressive who get it. To be tenacious and knowledgeable helps."[2] Such persons almost invariably have been members of the dominant Anglo culture.

The corollary proposition to the adage, namely that water runs away from the poor and powerless, is less well understood and almost unstudied. This book examines the relationship between water and poverty in an arid region where throughout human history, control over scarce water resources has caused conflict. The book addresses two questions. (1) How is water important to the rural poor in the Southwest—principally Indians and Hispanics? (2) What realistic, water-based strategies offer the best hope for advancing the interests of the rural poor?

The response to these questions consists of three interrelated propositions. First, there is an extremely strong bond between water and the cultural values of the rural poor. For this reason, perceived threats to their water interests evoke from the poor a vigorous and emotional reaction. Successfully gaining or preserving control over water contributes to the improvement of their general welfare by affirming and fulfilling cultural values.

Second, effectively participating in water policy in order to control water will strengthen the capacity of the poor to advance their general interest within the larger society of which they are a part. Although water may not be a unique vehicle to build

1

capacity, water provides a major opportunity for the rural poor because it so strongly motivates participation. Further, fundamental changes are occurring in western water institutions and policies, which provide openings not before available whereby the the rural poor can insert their interests into water resources policy making. By collectively acting to promote and preserve water values, the poor have an opportunity to build capability to improve their condition in areas beyond simply realizing water values.

Third, the economic condition of poor rural people can be improved by water-based strategies that offer economic benefits as well as being culturally compatible. Solid evidence suggests that the water development strategy most acceptable and desirable to rural communities involves irrigated agriculture. Although there is no guarantee that agricultural strategies that build upon community desires and values will succeed, strategies that ignore these values are certainly doomed. The obstacles to the development of a successful and profitable irrigation economy are substantial, as shown herein. None are insurmountable, however, given time, will, and judicious assistance commensurate with the challenge.

Empirical evidence for the proposition comes from information gathered in two in-depth case studies of particularly poor rural communities. Hispanics in the Upper Rio Grande are the focus of the first case study presented in Chapters 4 through 8. The Tohono O'odham Nation (formerly the Papago Tribe) of southern Arizona near Tucson is discussed in Chapters 9 through 14. In advance of the case studies, Chapters 2 and 3 entitled, respectively, "The Rising Commodity Value and View of Water" and "The Community Value of Water" describe and analyze major economic, political, legal, and cultural forces at work in the reshaping of the region's water institutions. Essentially, these chapters present the context within which the rural poor must evolve a water-based strategy through their preferences, decisions, and actions.

Chapter 15 compares and distinguishes the two case studies, drawing lessons from each for the conclusions presented in Chapter 16. The remainder of this introductory chapter presents a brief historical and statistical portrait of the rural poor in the region with emphasis on their relationship to water. It also justifies the selection of the Upper Rio Grande Hispanics and the Tohono O'odham as examples of rural poverty.

Water Development and the Rural Poor

During the development period that has characterized western water affairs over the last one hundred years, the rural poor of the region neither extensively benefited from, nor effectively participated in, decisions involving river compacts, dam or reclamation project construction, or most other major water events. In a number of important respects, developmental activities have actually been injurious to their interests.

Historically, the development of the surface streams of the region, particularly the Colorado, was made possible by the existence of a powerful, politically skilled coalition that could translate its development aims into federal dollars by making use of a reclamation ethic having substantial national support.[3] Although debate was often acrimonious and contention frequent, there was a pervasive desire throughout the region to harness the rivers with dams, generate cheap hydroelectric power, and construct aqueducts to transport water to irrigation projects and population centers.

Neither the coalition nor the developmental activity it fostered represented the full range of regional constituencies. One conspicuous exception may be collectively termed the rural poor and includes both Indians and Hispanics. For Indians a clear symbol of their absence from the coalition is contained in the language of the 1922 Colorado River Compact, one of the elder water institutions in the region. Despite the fact that Indian "reserved rights" had been given judicial recognition by the United States Supreme Court during the first decade of the century,[4] the Indian tribes of the Colorado were not included in the 1922 negotiations. The resulting compact, which divided the flow of the Colorado between its upper and lower basins and opened the door to construction of Hoover Dam and the development of the river, sidestepped potential Indian rights with the language, "Nothing in this compact shall be construed as affecting the obligations of the United States of America to

Indian tribes."[5] Though the negotiators were aware of potential tribal claims, the Indians were not included in this most-basic developmental decision on the Colorado.

The Hispanics of the Upper Rio Grande in southern Colorado and northern New Mexico have, in large measure, also not been party to the developmental coalition. As a consequence, many water storage facilities and water delivery systems built in the Upper Rio Grande region have been mainly for the benefit of extraregional interests.[6] Many of the Hispanic community irrigation systems (acequias) suffer from inadequate earthen and brush diversion works, which wash out with spring floods, and from inadequate waterflow in the latter months of the growing season because there is insufficient storage capacity to hold some of the spring runoff for the drier months ahead.

In those locations in which development has proceeded without the participation of the rural poor, they not only failed to share in benefits but their interests have frequently been damaged. For example, it is politically more difficult for tribes to implement their court-granted "paper rights" and obtain "wet water" when all of the water supply in a basin is already being used. An even more extreme example has occurred in the Upper Rio Grande in which two of the oldest water-using societies in the nation, Pueblos and Hispanics, have been pitted against one another in the wake of developmental decisions on the Rio Grande, as will be described more fully in Chapter Five. There are few exceptions to the general rule of the water development period, which ignored or further impoverished the poor. Even the largest Indian water development, the Navajo Irrigation Project, followed a tortuous funding path that lagged far behind its politically negotiated, non-Indian counterpart, the San Juan–Chama diversion project.[7]

Opportunity and Challenge in the Management Era

Now, just as some leaders of the rural poor have acquired facility with the rules of the development game, western water institutions and policies are fundamentally changing. In the words of former-governor Bruce Babbitt of Arizona, "The old institutions are crumbling."[8] This change is most pronounced in the

Southwest, where the surface water supplies are essentially fully appropriated and many groundwater aquifers are being mined, while economies and the population continue to grow. Coupled with declining federal developmental funding, these factors have created strong pressures that are shifting the region's water institutions away from their almost exclusive focus on development. Increasingly, the functions performed by these institutions are more accurately described as *water management,* in which conservation, reallocation, and quality preservation and improvement assume greater importance relative to traditional development activity.

As the region begins the transition into the management era,[9] an important opportunity exists to include the rural poor in discussion processes that will reshape the region's water institutions, policies, and events. Effective participation is essential not only from the standpoint of the rural poor themselves but also in the interest of the larger society, within which those excluded become destabilizing forces. The consequence of tribes having been left out of past water development decisions is the increasingly costly and time-consuming litigation and negotiation over Indian water rights that currently clog the courts and political arena. Everyone suffers: business and governmental leaders fear the extensive delays caused by protracted dispute; Indian leaders fear yet another assault on a valuable natural resource they regard as part of their heritage and legal right.

The inequity that many rural poor perceive as having taken place in the development period has left strong feelings of bitterness and suspicion. They are no longer willing to remain neglected constituencies. In the Upper Rio Grande, for example, recent decades have seen a proposed dam and conservancy district defeated by Hispanics,[10] Indian water rights asserted in a protracted and emotional court battle,[11] and resistance to market sales of water rights by Hispanics.[12]

These clashes are just part of a general struggle over water that is taking place between the rural poor and municipal and industrial interests in the region. Less-developed, traditional cultures and communities, whose capacity to act effectively in modern circumstances is just being forged, are confronting the often-aggressive, more-affluent communities, whose values and objectives are secure.

We believe that despite the strong tensions surrounding water issues, which wax and wane with the advent and resolution of particular disputes, there is a growing opportunity for both the political and economic interests of the rural poor to be effectively inserted into water decision processes. That assessment rests on four factors: (1) the strength and extent of their claim on water, (2) the increased possibility for innovation during a period of fundamental institutional change, (3) the increased openness of the water decision process that is occurring coupled with the arrival of a new generation of water leaders, and (4) most importantly, the growing skill and determination with which their interests are asserted. All of these factors are extensively discussed and illustrated in the chapters ahead.

Whether the opportunity will be successfully pursued remains to be determined. The battles over water have been and will be arduous. The responsibility for articulating and asserting the water-related values and interests of the rural poor in the Southwest ultimately rests with those communities and their leaders. External assistance, judiciously directed, can be useful, and societal receptivity to these values is essential. This book is intended to aid in the process of change by analytically bringing together the internal opinion and preferences of selected groups of the rural poor regarding water with the external reality of the formidable political and economic forces at work in the reshaping of the institutional structure for water management in the region and nation. It is intended to assist in the struggle and change by informing all parties to it.

The Rural Poor in the Southwest

Just who are the rural poor in this region? First, we must give some context to the meaning and occurrence of poverty. Low income is clearly an element in the poverty condition, but as many authorities have noted, it is not relative economic status alone that signals poverty. Instead, poverty also connotes an inability on the part of people to exercise substantial control over their own lives and to cope effectively with outside pressures. Poor people often lack the level of education necessary to perform successfully in complex modern society. Very frequently poor people also suffer substantial social and political barriers when their poverty condition is combined with an accompanying status as racial or religious minorities. For these reasons an identification of rural poverty should be based on criteria including powerlessness as well as economic statistics. Such documentation is provided as part of the case studies. However, for purposes of this initial overview only published statistics, principally economic, are used.

Based on economics, the rural poor in the Southwest can be identified as principally consisting of Indians, Upper Rio Grande rural Hispanics, and some Hispanic populations along the U.S.-Mexico border. Of course, there are poor Anglo farmers, and not all Indians are poor. But on an income basis Indians and rural Hispanics are the main groups constituting the rural poor. This conclusion was reached in a series of steps. First, available census data involving county aggregates were examined. These aggregates hide intracounty variation but generally yield valid comparisons between counties. Two income criteria, county per capita income and percentage of persons below the official poverty level, were used. The informal "rules of thumb" for designating a county as containing substantial poverty were (1) its per capita income was less than 75 percent of the 1979 U.S. designated percentage level of $9,411 reported by the 1980 Census; and (2) the percentage of persons living under the poverty level in the county was 20 percent or more.[13] The map shows those counties with a substantial degree of poverty as identified by this method. Table 1.1 contains data on per capita income and percentage of persons below poverty level for these counties.

When demographic data for these counties are reviewed, persons below poverty level are found to be heavily Indian and rural Hispanic, although exceptions do exist. All of the three counties in Arizona identified by the above method are in the northeastern part of the state, where the huge Navajo reservation dominates census statistics. One of the two Utah poverty

Table 1.1. Counties of the Southwest Containing
a Substantial Degree of Poverty

	Per Capita Income, 1980[a]	Percentage of Population Below Official Poverty Level, 1979[b]
Arizona	$8,814	13.2%
Apache County	5,437	40.0
Coconino County	7,040	20.4
Navajo County	6,229	29.7
Utah	7,681	10.3
San Juan County	5,092	31.9
Wayne County	6,354	22.3
Colorado	10,033	7.4
Conejos County	4,139	30.4
Costilla County	5,967	36.1
Huerfano County	6,177	20.2
Los Animas County	7,056	20.4
Saguache County	5,698	26.8
New Mexico	7,878	17.6
Catron County	5,171	23.0
Dona Ana County	6,328	22.7
Guadalupe County	5,691	30.5
Luna County	6,985	23.3
McKinley County	6,032	36.8
Mora County	4,473	38.3
Rio Arriba County	5,588	28.3
San Miguel County	4,894	30.8
Socorro County	5,366	29.6
Taos County	6,128	27.5
Torrance County	6,016	23.3
United States	9,411	13.0

SOURCES: [a]Bureau of Economic Analysis, *Survey of Current Business*, vol. 62, no. 4 (Washington, D.C.: U.S. Department of Commerce, April 1982).
[b]Bureau of the Census, *1980 Census of Population*, Summary Tape file 3, Table 50—State Summaries (Washington, D.C.: U.S. Department of Commerce).

counties (San Juan County, Utah) is also located in Navajoland. The other Utah poverty county is quite small, with less than two thousand people.

The poverty counties in Colorado are all in south central Colorado, mainly in the upper Rio Grande drainage. These rural Colorado counties are characterized by high proportions of Hispanics. More than 40 percent of the population of each is of Spanish origin, and for two of the counties the proportion exceeds 60 percent. New Mexico has twelve poverty counties, and five of these are in north central New Mexico, in the Upper Rio Grande drainage. All five of the northern New Mexico counties have over 65 percent of their population of Hispanic origin. Another New Mexico county, McKinley, contains a substantial segment of the Navajo reservation and population. A portion of rural New Mexico poverty is also located in the southern part of the state. Table 1.2 provides additional social and demographic information on all of these counties. All of the column headings are self-explanatory with the exception of the three health indices, which are all alcohol related. Each of the indices[14] is a standardized normal variate that indicates a relatively strong degree of alcohol abuse by higher, positive scores and a relatively weak degree by low, negative scores.

Poverty among Indian tribes is obscured by county-level statistics because only the Navajo are large enough to figure prominently in these statistics. For some demographic comparability with the county population totals in Table 1.2, the data in Table 1.3 provide information on Indian population at the state level for each of the four southwestern states. Of the reservation Indians, 110,000 are Navajo, 18,000 are Pueblo, and 7,000 are Tohono O'odham.[15]

Because this book is concerned with the relationship between poverty and water in the Southwest, the populations of particular interest are those associated with substantial existing water use or having substantial unrealized claims to water as is the case with many Indian tribes. For that reason the populations of interest are the Hispanics in the counties of

Table 1.2. Social and Demographic Information for Counties

	Composite Index	Chronic Health Index	Casualty Index	Population Distribution by Race (%)				Spanish Origin[a] (%)	Education Distribution (%)[b]					1981 Unemployment Rate
				White	Black	Indian	Other		0–8	H.S. 1–3	H.S. 4	Coll. 1–3	Coll. 4+	
Arizona	.54	.38	.38	82.4	2.8	5.6	9.2	16.2	15.0	12.7	34.3	20.6	17.4	6.2
Apache	4.63	2.88	3.72	22.8	.5	74.9	1.7	3.8	39.2	11.5	24.9	14.0	10.4	21.5
Coconino	1.00	.29	1.24	65.6	1.7	27.9	4.8	9.8	16.1	9.5	30.4	20.8	23.2	8.4
Navajo	1.81	1.32	1.23	48.1	.9	47.5	3.5	6.7	25.6	14.7	32.1	16.4	11.2	15.2
Utah	.09	.01	.08	94.6	.6	1.3	3.5	4.1	7.0	12.9	36.0	24.2	19.9	5.9
San Juan	1.35	.36	1.69	52.4	.1	45.7	1.8	3.5	28.6	12.6	28.1	16.4	14.3	8.1
Wayne	−1.30	− .75	−1.17	98.7	.1	.9	.3	1.3	11.8	16.6	40.0	18.8	12.9	8.8
Colorado	.11	.04	.10	90.0	3.5	.6	5.9	11.8	10.6	10.8	34.6	21.1	23.0	5.5
Conejos	.74	.45	.57	58.9	*	.5	40.5	61.2	32.9	15.1	29.3	12.9	9.7	14.2
Costilla	1.10	.13	1.50	71.4	.1	*	28.5	77.5	38.0	16.1	25.7	10.1	10.1	17.8
Huerfano	1.04	.44	1.17	83.4	.5	.5	15.6	44.0	34.6	12.9	28.8	12.5	11.3	8.8
Los Animas	1.35	.91	.97	87.4	.4	.5	11.7	43.7	27.3	11.3	32.2	17.9	11.3	7.6
Saguache	.08	.10	− .05	70.5	.2	1.2	28.0	41.2	28.0	12.7	33.1	14.9	11.2	8.9
New Mexico	1.65	1.08	1.21	75.0	1.8	8.1	15.0	36.6	17.7	13.5	34.1	17.1	17.6	7.3
Catron	.64	− .93	2.44	89.1	*	1.5	9.1	28.7	19.4	19.0	32.5	15.6	13.5	12.7
Dona Ana	.05	.06	− .06	78.2	1.7	*	19.4	52.1	23.9	11.0	30.0	15.8	19.3	7.8
Guadalupe	4.28	4.30	2.16	82.6	*	*	17.1	82.7	33.5	17.6	32.6	9.0	7.3	10.5
Luna	1.68	.84	1.57	85.6	1.6	*	12.3	39.4	23.9	19.2	35.6	10.7	10.7	9.3
McKinley	8.86	5.81	6.45	25.9	*	65.7	7.8	13.5	33.7	15.2	28.8	11.7	10.7	10.1
Mora	2.99	1.77	2.46	62.2	*	*	37.6	86.6	39.6	16.3	28.1	6.1	9.9	31.4
Rio Arriba	4.53	3.59	2.85	44.4	*	11.4	44.1	74.4	29.4	14.2	35.7	10.5	10.1	18.3
San Miguel	2.94	2.82	1.31	74.4	*	*	24.8	81.4	30.7	13.5	27.2	13.4	15.3	10.6
Socorro	2.43	1.16	2.31	81.9	*	9.9	7.8	46.7	23.4	13.0	33.8	14.1	15.7	8.0
Taos	1.82	1.10	1.50	52.8	*	6.4	40.6	69.1	21.4	15.9	32.4	17.0	13.4	14.3
Torrance	1.93	1.04	1.66	73.5	*	*	25.6	41.1	25.6	16.0	39.1	9.8	9.5	3.1

Sources: National Institute on Alcohol Abuse and Alcoholism. *County Alcohol Problem Indicators 1975–1977* (Washington. D.C.: NIAAA); Bureau of the Census, *1980 Census of Population*. (Washington. D.C.: U.S. Department of Commerce). Dept. of Economic Security, Labor Market Information, Research & Analysis. Phoenix, Ariz: Dept. of Employment Security, *Non-Agricultural Wage & Salary*. Salt Lake City, Utah: Division of Employment & Training. Labor Market Information Section. Denver, Colo: Employment Security Dept.. *Non-Agricultural Wage & Salary*, Table A. Albuquerque. N.M.
[a]Persons were listed as Spanish origin if they identified their ancestry as Mexican. Mexican-American. Chicano. Puerto Rican or Cuban.
[b]Respondents were 25 years old or older.
*Less than 0.01%.

Table 1.3. American Indian Data for the Southwest, 1979

| | No. of American Indians | | |
	Urban	Rural	Total
New Mexico	30,563	74,431	104,994
Arizona	47,301	103,310	150,611
Utah	9,355	8,800	18,155
Colorado	14,861	5,152	20,013
TOTAL:	102,080	191,693	293,773

| | Per Capita Income of American Indians | | |
	Urban	Rural	Total
New Mexico	$3,617	$2,698	$2,972
Arizona	3,716	2,360	2,796
Utah	3,597	2,556	3,126
Colorado	5,508	4,743	5,317
TOTAL:	$3,936	$2,565	$3,051

| | American Indians in Households with 1979 Income below Poverty Level (%) | | |
	Urban	Rural	Total
New Mexico	28.7	41.5	37.6
Arizona	31.3	49.8	44.0
Utah	29.2	43.9	36.3
Colorado	21.8	27.4	23.3
TOTAL:	29.0	45.6	39.8

SOURCE: Bureau of the Census, *1980 Census of Population*; General Social and Economic Characteristics (Washington, D.C.: U.S. Department of Commerce). See separate volumes for each of the four states.

north central New Mexico and south central Colorado and the Indians. The two case studies identified above were drawn from these populations. The Tohono O'odham Nation was selected from among southwestern tribes principally because of their urban proximity and recently concluded negotiations that provided a partial settlement of their water right claims.

The Control and Use of Water by the Rural Poor

The water rights system of the Southwest is highly complex. Moreover, it treats Indian tribes differently from rural Hispanics. A brief historical review explains how the system evolved. For hunters and gatherers[16] who moved from water source to water source in the region for thousands of years, water use customs were relatively simple. Subsequent agricultural settlement, particularly during Spanish colonialization (1540–1821), gave rise to the need for a system of enforceable rights to the use of water. Formally, the Spanish colonial system honored grants of land made on parchments issued under authority of the king, and the right to reasonable water use was attendant to the land. In practice, disputes over water use were seldom resolved by courts and officials on the basis of written title alone but also took account of prior use, need, third party rights, intent, governmental priorities, municipal and Pueblo preferences, and notions of equity and common good.[17] Both the Spanish and the later Mexican (1822–1846) reign saw water allocated in a process balancing formal title claims with people's needs and expectations.[18]

Rights created under Spanish and Mexican rule were recognized by the United States in a protocol accompanying the 1848 Treaty of Guadalupe Hidalgo. Congress did not prescribe a water rights system for the region, leaving the territorial legislatures and courts free to declare a public interest in water, while rushing to make rights private through the rule of prior appropriation (first-in-time, first-in-right).[19] Federal rights in navigable water were announced only occasionally, and the legal doctrine of reserved water rights for Indians was not pronounced by the U.S. Supreme Court until 1908,[20] long after most Indian reservations had been created. Similar rights for reserved federal lands, such as National Forests and National Parks, were recognized even later, in 1963.[21]

Several strata of water rights thus were laid down in the settlement of the Southwest and persist today: (1) pre-1848 rights of use officially granted or awarded under Spanish and Mexican rule, (2) post-1848 appropriative rights perfected under territorial and state law, (3) sundry rights asserted by states over their public waters, (4) federal navigational and reserved rights, and (5) Indian reserved rights. Hispanics hold both pre- and post-1848 rights. Indians on reservations variously hold or claim pre-1848 rights (e.g., Pueblo or aboriginal) and reserved rights. As mentioned, many of the Indian rights have not been quantified or adjudicated, leaving considerable uncertainty as to their extent.[22]

Although water use differs considerably among different groups of the rural poor, there are some constants. Agriculture is everywhere a primary consumptive user, though the type of agriculture varies from cotton in southern Arizona to alfalfa in northern New Mexico. The significance to the rural poor of the agriculture for which water is used invariably is more than simple economic benefit. Agriculture is an important part of lifestyle, even though it may be a part-time activity. The agricultural enterprise attaches indigenous people to a place and provides a link to the past. Even the part-time farmer gains a sense of security and independence from the predominantly Anglo world in which he or she may be employed. The relationship of water to human values that transcend economic returns is a subject developed more fully in chapters that follow. However, the narrower economic or commodity perspective on water is currently on the ascendancy, and it is to this perspective we turn in Chapter 2.

CHAPTER 2

The Rising Commodity Value
and View of Water

The Changing Rules of the Water Game

Rapid population growth has been the salient social feature of the Southwest in modern times. Although the pace of this growth has ebbed and flowed from decade to decade, the general trend is pronounced. The most recent decennial census (1970–1980) reported substantially larger percentage gains in population for Arizona (53.5 percent), Colorado (30.9 percent), New Mexico (28.2 percent), and Utah (37.9 percent) than for the United States (11.4 percent) as a whole.[1]

One consequence of this population growth and the associated economic growth has been a sharp increase in water consumption for municipal (public) and industrial purposes as seen in Table 2.1. Although the largest consumer of water

Table 2.1. Southwestern Water Consumption by Use, 1960–1980

	Water Consumed (millions of gallons/day)		
	1960	*1970*	*1980*
Public supply	237	453	899
Rural uses	98	158	137
Irrigation	11,300	14,400	11,700
Self-supplied industry	100	299	529
TOTAL	11,735	15,310	13,265

SOURCES: K. A. Mackichan and J. C. Kannerer, *Estimated Use of Water in the U.S., 1960*, U.S. Geological Survey Circular 456 (Washington, D.C.: U.S. Department of Interior); C. R. Murray and E. B. Reeves, *Estimated Use of Water in the U.S., 1970*, U.S. Geological Survey Circular 676 (Washington, D.C.: U.S. Department of Interior); W. B. Solley, E. B. Chase, and W. B. Mann IV, *Estimated Use of Water in the U.S., 1980*, U.S. Geological Survey Circular 1001 (Washington, D.C.: U.S. Department of Interior).

in the region continues to be irrigated agriculture, its share in regional consumption dropped significantly from 1970 to 1980. In terms of actual control over water, the shift away from agriculture is probably even more emphatic, though there is no documentation of ownership or contractual control. Many municipalities and industrial users purchase water rights whenever they are available as a general policy. Such rights often continue to be exercised for agricultural purposes pending actual need for municipal or industrial use.[2]

Habitually state and local governments and private firms have sought to meet prospective demand for additional water by securing and developing previously untapped supplies. The regional coalition described in Chapter 1 was forged largely for the purpose of developing new supplies and that goal held the coalition together despite its substantial internal tensions. In an arid region, it commonly does not take much growth to exhaust the immediately contiguous water supplies, making long-distance water importation necessary. Yet the mountainous terrain of the Southwest also makes interbasin transfers of water quite expensive. Therefore, the development of new water supplies has relied heavily on federal funding to build storage dams on the Colorado River and its tributaries and aqueducts to the coastal cities of southern California, to the urbanized front range of Colorado, and into the Rio Grande basin to serve Albuquerque and adjacent uses. Still under construction are the Central Arizona Project, designed to serve Phoenix and Tucson, and the Central Utah Project, to facilitate use of Utah's principal share of the coalition's benefits.[3]

Now, however, the burdens placed upon new supply solutions have grown almost unsurmountably. Although the strong desire for new supplies is still present and imaginative schemes for securing new supplies can still be conjured up, two fundamental factors have substantially changed. The first is the increased geographic distance to new supplies, and the second is the diminished fiscal capacity and willingness of the Congress to underwrite the continued development of new water supplies for the region. Full appropriation has spread from the immediate environs of growth areas to adjacent basins. The distance to untapped supplies is now very great. Both the Colorado and Rio Grande are essentially fully committed, probably even overappropriated in terms of long-term, sustainable flow. New supplies to the region would allegedly have to tap water surplus basins such as the Columbia, around which initial defensive perimeters have already been drawn.

Even if massive, long distance, interbasin transfer schemes were politically feasible, the sheer cost of such plans would certainly cause them to founder in the near term on the shoals of reduced federal financing. The Carter "hit list" of 1977,[4] which initially marked a number of major western water projects for extinction, may in hindsight be considered as a warning shot across the bow of the "water business as usual" practice of logrolling and mutual accommodation among Congressmen supporting desired projects in each other's districts. With the massive federal deficits of the eighties, continued federal funding has become very difficult to secure, even for those projects far along in construction. Earlier in this century the regional coalition, in pushing for federal funding, could tap a shared national desire to "make the desert bloom." In current times, however, contention over perceived regional inequities in federal expenditures has essentially eliminated the power of this argument. Midwesterners, faced with the decline in many basic industries in their region, do not feel much sympathy for further subsidization of "Sunbelt" water projects.[5]

Faced with these new realities, the extensive institutional machinery that conducts the Southwest's water business has already begun adapting, as have a number of its political leaders. In order to assess adequately possible water strategies for the rural poor in the Southwest, we must describe this changing water context so as to see strategies in relation to the structure that is emerging rather than that which has been.

The Rising Commodity Value of Water

While water in an arid region is an emotional symbol, it is also a physical commodity of considerable importance to material prosperity in the region. As regional supplies have become committed and water demands have continued to rise, the economic value of water has increased, in some cases sharply and dramatically. As long as new supplies were readily available and the capital investment federally financed, it was easier and cheaper to apply for and receive a new appropriative right to part of a streamflow or to pump from groundwater stocks than to try to bid away existing rights from already established uses. When the new supply option is closed, or closing, as is happening in most regional subbasins, new demands where legally permitted are met through the sale and transfer of water rights from one use and user to another.[6]

In fully appropriated basins under continuing stress in New Mexico, Colorado, and Utah, sales of water rights have become relatively frequent, expensive, and critical. In the Northern Colorado Conservancy District, prices bid or asked-for shares to water from the Colorado–Big Thompson project are publicly posted as part of a practically proficient marketplace for water. Water right prices in some New Mexico subbasins have soared. Not long ago the perpetual right to consume one acre-foot of water annually sold for as little as $150 in basins containing uncommitted water, as the San Juan recently did. In other subbasins such as the Santa Fe area and the Gila, prices for a comparable right have reached the vicinity of $10,000 or more.[7] Irrigated agriculture will eventually be "cannibalized" by reliance upon laissez-faire markets for reallocating water, by one judge's prediction.[8]

In Arizona, the transfer process has been more cumbersome since water rights cannot be sold separately from the land. Yet even here water has moved out of agriculture to municipal and industrial use, the latter generally much more economically valuable than most agricultural uses, even though land must be purchased along with the water right.

Individualized farmers who hold perfected rights to water may be monetarily rewarded for this increasing value of water in the marketplace. A one-hundred-acre farm with minimal rights to 1½ acre-feet of consumptive use per acre of irrigated land can command $150,000 for its water rights at a price of $1,000 per acre-foot. At a price of $5,000 per acre-foot of water right, water rights on the same farm are work $750,000. Even ranchers whose land contains oil or natural gas frequently view their water rights as potentially their most valuable asset.

Market-driven reallocation of water among users can encounter strong opposition. For instance, past subsidies to irrigated agriculture carry built-in notions of inequity. It is inequitable to many people for a farmer who has benefited from public subsidies to profit, perhaps handsomely, from the increased value of water in the marketplace. Arizona exemplifies the counterforce contained within this sentiment in its recently adopted major reformulation of its groundwater code. The new code places strong reliance in meeting its objectives on governmental regulation and planning rather than on the marketplace. At least one contributing factor to this policy choice was the concern that "farmers would be raising martinis in southern California rather than crops in Arizona" if the marketplace should predominate.

Further opposition to the marketplace allocation of water springs from quite different sources. As elsewhere in the country, farming is considered a "way of life," whose proponents protect against demise or diminution. Many farmers within the Elephant Butte Irrigation District in New Mexico oppose applications by the city of El Paso, Texas, to groundwater within New Mexico[9] even though interrelated surface and groundwater hydrology would, under New Mexico's regulatory regime, enhance the economic value of the farmers' surface rights. Paraphrasing one farmer, "I'm just as interested in money as the next man, but I'm also interested in preserving this farm and the way of life that goes with it." Such sentiment reveals a community value of water, as we term it, which is explored in the next chapter.

Despite opposition, the marketplace value of water is increasing as a result of growing demand for water weighed against relatively fixed physical quantities (at least for the time being). Although this trend may vary in degree among regional subbasins and be subject to cyclical fluctuations, it is almost certain to continue as long as the region itself continues to grow demographically and economically. Some have suggested that limited water supply may serve to restrict regional growth. Yet extensive analysis of the regional economy and water supply emphatically concludes that short of a severe and prolonged drought, water will *not* be a constraint to regional economic growth in the coming decades.[10] Incrementally or dramatically, as in prolonged drought,[11] continued movement of water from agricultural to municipal and industrial usage can be expected.

The pace of change is more problematic than the more certain direction of change. The market pressure on agriculture's use of water is strong and definite, but the process of change will occur over decades or longer. A little irrigation water can go a long way toward meeting municipal demand. A one-hundred-acre farm will amply supply a municipal population of 1,200 people or more. Only a portion of the over 13 million acre-feet of water consumed in irrigation in 1980 would have to be converted to municipal use to meet growing demand. Various factors[12] suggest that the rate of decline in irrigated agriculture may not be as precipitous as a superficial projection of the regional growth rate might suggest.

The shift of water away from agriculture has significant implications for the rural poor who are rooted in agriculture. Further, these consequences are amplified by complementary trends in the judicial and political arenas.

The Rising Commodity View of Water

The Judiciary

At the same time as the marketplace is placing growing value on water as a commodity, the judiciary has changed perspective. Recent court decisions have found that water is almost exclusively and strictly a commodity to be governed by economic criteria. This shift can only be termed *fundamental* in terms of effect upon existing western water institutions, which have had different social and political basis.

The foremost example of the ascending judicial view of water as commodity is the 1982 United States Supreme Court decision in *Sporhase v. Nebraska*,[13] which declared (1) water to be a commodity subject to interstate commerce clause scrutiny and (2) the public ownership of water asserted by most western state statutes and constitutions to be a "legal fiction." The Court did express some awareness of the importance of water in an arid region and ostensibly qualified its opinion by suggesting that a state conceivably could muster public welfare arguments supporting a complete ban on exports of water from within its boundaries. Yet subsequent lower court decisions have narrowly interpreted this qualification in striking down a New Mexico statute restricting out-of-state applications for groundwater from New Mexico.[14]

The *Sporhase* decision has made an interstate market for water and water rights at least conceptually possible. Interests in more developed states may be able to lease or buy water rights in adjacent states that are less developed. The *Sporhase* decision has undercut state sovereignty over water within its boundaries, previously a principal institutional support for western water administration. State sovereignty over interstate streams had long been somewhat qualified by (1) negotiated and congressionally ratified compacts dividing the flow among the states involved or (2) equitable apportionment decrees handed down by the Court in interstate litigation.[15] Otherwise, however, state control over the water stocks and flows within their boundaries was assumed.

Even equitable apportionment no longer appears to be a judicially acceptable defense against interstate transfers of water rights. The Court affirmed established New Mexico uses in *Colorado v. New Mexico II*,[16] an equitable apportionment decision on the Vermejo River, which flows in both states. Nevertheless, it left the door open to a future reallocation of water between the competing states should Colorado successfully propose a bona fide use of water whose economic benefit outweighed the economic loss to New Mexico. Instead of establishing certainty of ownership as apportionment decrees of the past had at least appeared to do, the Vermejo decision suggests a flexible apportionment doctrine that may subsequently reallocate the disputed water based on economic criteria. It seems likely that the Court would support a purchase of water rights in New Mexico by a Colorado organization for use in Colorado.

Counterarguments remain. Defenders of compacts point to the congressional ratification process as protection against interstate commerce clause scrutiny. They argue that Congress implicitly gives states approval to withhold water from interstate commerce when it ratifies an interstate water apportionment compact. A similar case is made that federal water project legislation, such as the Boulder Canyon Project Act affecting the states in the lower basin of the Colorado, implicitly empowers states to ban water exports. Although the U.S. Supreme Court has yet to resolve such issues, test cases are in the making. Recently, the San Diego County Water Authority paid ten thousand dollars to a private company, the Galloway Group,[17] in the Upper Colorado River Basin as an option on a proposed leasing arrangement that would make a substantial quantity of Upper Basin water in Colorado, Utah, and Wyoming available for use in San Diego County. The legal and political obstacles to such an agreement are formidable. Certainly the framers of the 1922 Colorado Compact, long considered a fixed part of the Colorado's institutional machinery, did not envision a transfer that would allow water apportioned to the upper basin to be used in the lower basin. Such a transfer would circumvent various elements of the "Law of the River." Regardless of its outcome, the San Diego example illustrates that seemingly immutable institutional barriers such as compacts may be vulnerable to ingenious schemes.

Recent developments concerning Indian water rights further illustrate judicial proclivity toward the commodity perspective. In the 1963 landmark decision *Arizona v. California*,[18] the Supreme Court affirmed the Special Master's concept of practicably irrigable acreage (p.i.a.) as a means of quantifying Indian claims to water. (A Special Master is a judge appointed by a court—U.S. Supreme Court or lower—to hear testimony on technical matters such as water litigation.) As originally applied, that concept required a determination of the total acreage on a reservation that could practicably be irrigated based on a technical engineering and horticultural analysis. A more recent Special Master in the continuing *Arizona v. California* proceedings[19] sought for the first time to introduce economic considerations into the p.i.a. criterion. Would the benefits from irrigating a given tract outweigh the costs incurred? Although in 1983 the Supreme Court refused to accept this interpretation and recalculate practicably irrigable acreage, citing the need for finality, Indian claims may ultimately be limited by economic criteria. The implication for tribal water claims is substantial.

Although the judiciary has tended recently to reinforce the commodity perspective on water in the marketplace, the long-term trend is less clear. On the one hand, the judicial trend in water matters is certainly consistent with current national policy and international affairs. In the seventies and eighties the combination of an increasingly competitive international economy and declining real personal income has created a general atmosphere of concern about the nation's ability to achieve material goals. That concern has fueled a drive toward improved productivity and a tendency to make judgments more closely on economic grounds, even at the expense of other values.

On the other hand, the Court has always seen its principal function as determining equity. The judiciary, after all, initially asserted the concept of reserved water rights for Indian tribes. The qualifying language used by the Court in both *Sporhase* and *Colorado v. New Mexico II* suggests a continuing recognition of equity concerns. A vague sensitivity to the public welfare concerns of arid states was exhibited in *Sporhase*, and in the *New Mexico* case the Court dismissed what it termed a "speculative" use of water as proposed by the Colorado firm that sought the water. Although no one can be certain, perhaps what is occurring is a reinforcement of the marketplace to the extent that the Court seeks only to avoid waste and encourage productive use of the scarce resource. If this is the case, perhaps equity instruments such as compacts and political apportionments of navigable waters by Congress are likely to be reaffirmed rather than overturned or circumvented.

Governments

Each of the states within the region is still preoccupied with completing planned development of new water supplies or, in the New Mexico case, defending state sovereignty over in-state water. Arizona's first political priority remains the completion of the Central Arizona Project (CAP), which includes bringing that aqueduct down to Tucson from Phoenix. Utah is preoccupied with the completion of the Central Utah Project (CUP).[20] Colorado has an undeveloped portion of the state's compacted share of the Colorado River, which has yet to be put to beneficial use. Unless developed, that share will continue to flow to users in the Lower Basin. A priority political concern in Colorado, therefore, is the capture of benefits from this entitled share. The San Diego County Water Authority leasing proposal offers one speculative possibility for gaining revenue from this share,[21] though state government officially expressed strong reservations about that particular proposal.

In New Mexico there are some smaller projects such as Hooker Dam, part of the larger CAP, which have not yet been constructed although they are authorized. However, New Mexico's principal concern in recent years has been directed toward defensive efforts associated with the Colorado claim on the Vermejo, El Paso's groundwater applications, and litigation with Texas over the Pecos, which, though compacted, is still disputed.

These political efforts in each state aimed at completing the development of the new supplies may be described as the "end game" of the old coalition. The task the states have set for themselves is to complete the desired projects with as much federal funding as the transition to the new rules will allow. Colorado is even devoting some effort to finishing the developmental tasks under the new rules if that can be managed. Preoccupied with completing the development of new supplies, the governments at the state level have not really focused on the new management era, except to the extent that circumstances have forced them. Thus, it is not possible to make a clear reading of just how the political process will ultimately treat the commodity view of water. However, there are a few leading examples that can be drawn upon, both from inside and outside the southwest region.

The *Arizona Groundwater Management Act of 1980* revolutionized the management of groundwater in Arizona by forcefully inserting state authority into the water allocation process in declining groundwater areas. The implementation of the act is still in its early stages, and so it is too soon to make a judgment about the institutional character of the system as it will finally take shape. However, two features of the new system are revealing with respect to water as a commodity. The first is the strong regulatory structure adopted. Rather than leaving the water reallocation process to the marketplace, the state designated critical groundwater areas (around Phoenix, around Tucson, and Pinal County) and established regulatory agencies called Active Management Areas (AMAs) with definite management goals. "The management goal for all AMAs, except Pinal, is safe yield by the year 2025. Safe yield is reached when groundwater withdrawals equal recharge, thereby eliminating overdraft."[22] To meet this goal, the AMAs have substantial regulatory power, including the capacity to set irrigation efficiencies for each farm unit in an AMA.

A second important feature of the management system from a commodity perspective is the attachment of water rights to land. In the Tucson AMA, for example, the agency has issued certificates recognizing Irrigation GFR (grandfathered rights) for approximately fifty-three thousand irrigated acres. Neither these rights nor others associated with farmland retired from irrigation in anticipation of a specific nonirrigation use can generally be sold separately from the land, though the use of GFRs can be changed.

The Groundwater Management Act has both its supporters and detractors, and there is no intention here of discussing its strengths and weaknesses nor of describing its provisions in detail. The significant conclusion instead is the existence of a political will in Arizona in favor of a governmental management structure. Water is not perceived strictly as an economic commodity whose allocation is to be left to the marketplace.[23]

The commodity view has fared differently in other western states. South Dakota recently embraced a market sale of water to a coal slurry consortium, Energy Transportation Systems Inc. (ETSI), whose plan, though now defunct, would have used substantial quantities of water to transport coal slurry from Wyoming to southern states. Wyoming itself was less receptive to overtures from ETSI, despite the fact that its coal would have been involved. Montana, torn between forces interested in repeating South Dakota's apparent coup and interests arguing that water had value to the state apart from strict economic benefits, created a special legislative subcommittee to gather information, consider arguments, and make recommendations. The subsequent report[24] led to enactment of legislation that establishes a water marketing capacity but qualifies its authority with respect to water for agriculture. ETSI, while it was alive, engendered a mixed reaction. Rather than helping to establish a clear trend in the political/governmental perspective on water, it has evoked strong conflict.

City governments are presented with different problems than those of states. The reality of water scarcity in the region has been most sharply encountered by a few of the region's municipalities. In particular, Tucson and Santa Fe have each faced at least one dimension of a water-scarce environment, so it is instructive to briefly consider the political perspective on water at this level of government.

An illuminating episode occurred in Tucson in 1976 when a "controlled growth" city council tried to substantially change and raise the city's water rate structure to reflect rising water related costs. Included among the changes were an increasing block rate structure and a lift charge to compensate for pumping water to those higher areas of the city in the foothills of the adjacent mountains. In the bitter battle that followed, the initiators of the rate increase and change were recalled, and a new council elected. Ironically, once it was installed and could more deliberately consider the situation, the new council accepted the necessity of the rate increase, though not the lift charge component. Tucson appears to have adjusted to higher water rates and declines in per capita water use, although overdraft continues as population rises. Whether, and at what social and environmental cost, groundwater overdraft will be controlled remains to be determined.[25]

Population growth in Santa Fe during the last several decades has outstripped the contiguous water supply of the Rio Grande tributary on which the city is located. As one consequence the privately owned utility serving the city has turned to the main stem of the Rio Grande for new water with a resulting high lift cost needed to bring the water up to Santa Fe's elevation. Conflict between the residents and the private utility over higher and higher rates has sharpened,[26] and the city has been exploring the possibility of buying the company with the hope that public ownership and control would produce more acceptable prices and service. The only vote on the question taken before 1986 rejected public ownership. The privately owned utility has adopted a new rate structure that charges residents in peripheral developments more than those in the central city, partly in response to central city rate-payers who complained about higher water rates due to the cost of serving outlying areas.[27]

What are the lessons from these governmental examples? Clearly there is substantial resistance to pricing water at commodity cost levels. Many old hands in western water affairs report a public aversion to having water priced at all. "It should be free just like the air." Yet with declining groundwater tables and increasing distances to new sources, cost increases become inevitable. The record at the municipal level suggests that initial resistance will give way to accommodation if the facts appear incontrovertible and after all alternatives such as changes in political control and public ownership of utilities have been explored. One signal of the future may be suggested by Arizona's state regulatory structure for managing groundwater. It may be that the public is going to insist on some degree of direct, public control of their water affairs rather than allowing private institutions such as markets to work largely unencumbered. Even the commodity perspective revealed by South Dakota in the ETSI case would support this tentative conclusion since the agreement was struck with state government at the highest levels, involving the governor and legislature directly. Yet the force of the marketplace is strong, and even the region's political leadership has begun turning in that direction.[28]

Pressure toward public decision making about water is further amplified by growing insistence upon openness in the water policy process. For most of the development period, decision making in water matters was left to the technicians and specialists. After all, a dominant coalition with a clear objective existed that was at least passively endorsed by the general public. With the rise of environmental concerns in the sixties and early seventies (e.g., the battle over proposed dams in the Grand Canyon), water issues began to occupy more and more of public attention in the Southwest. In the late seventies and eighties this process has continued with regard to water quality issues. Reinforcing the importance of governmental channels in water decisions, a broad array of interests now insist upon a voice in the policy-making process.

This chapter has focused almost exclusively on a strict view of water as a commodity, only briefly alluding to the emotional attitudes that treat water in more than utilitarian terms. Yet the symbolic importance of water is both profound and profoundly underestimated. Before considering the implications of current trends for the water strategies of the rural poor, the community value of water must be considered.

CHAPTER 3

The Community Value of Water
and Implications for the Rural Poor

Setting the Questions

In the Southwest, as in arid regions generally, water is a special resource. Because water is essential to the quality of life and also to a secure future, westerners place a value on water that transcends its material worth. Thus narrow pecuniary gain has not been the exclusive motivation underlying and sustaining the drive to capture and develop often enormously costly new water supplies. To be sure, there have been substantial profits to be made from these water development efforts, and the acquisition of new water supplies has made possible lucrative residential, commercial, and even agricultural development that would have been much more difficult, sometimes impossible, without the water projects. Yet to view the strong motivation toward water development only from an economic perspective is to ignore the deep-seated political and psychological factors involved.

Economists have frequently lamented the fact that many water projects fail to pass economic muster yet are funded and constructed anyway.[1] Arguably the federal financial support has made many projects more attractive to the region than they would have been in its absence. However, there are sufficient examples around of water projects funded exclusively through local or state sources to suggest that many projects would have been built even if the cost had not been spread nationally, albeit at a smaller scale and slower pace.[2]

The elemental objectives motivating water development strategies are secure ownership and some control over the future. In an arid region there is no more fundamental source of anxiety to those familiar with the natural environment than the prospect of water shortage. Although newcomers and urban dwellers may assume a water affluence based upon superficialities such as spouting fountains in residential developments and artificial ocean waves in recreational enterprises, natives and rural residents know that an extended drought may be as close as next spring, and even in years of good spring runoff, the summer and fall may be harsh. The assurance of a secure water future is a strongly held goal that is not much illuminated by a dollar calculus of costs and benefits. Consequently southwestern cities, industry, and agriculture have sought to gain control over whatever unused supplies of water might conceivably be had. Potential areas of origin have reacted with some anxiety. At one juncture in the funding history of the Central Arizona Project, for example, nervous congressional representatives from the Columbia River basin successfully attached a rider to a proposed bill prohibiting even studies by federal agencies of potential interbasin transfers from the Columbia to the Southwest.[3] No sooner did the moratorium on discussion expire than water project proposals sprang up once again, only to be silenced by a new amendment.

The role of water in establishing or maintaining a feeling of well-being results in a strong symbolic and emotional attachment. This *community value of water* is particularly strong among many Indians and rural Hispanics, as is documented in the case studies that follow. Their continued proximity to the natural environment and the insecurity of their cultures in modern circumstances make the presence of water crucial to their community well-being. This special attitude is sufficiently prevalent in all communities, however, that it compels examination as part of any effort by the rural poor, or others, to build a viable water strategy.

What evidence supports the assertion that water is a "special" resource, and what function does it serve other than contributing to material gain? If water is perceived in symbolic terms, what values does it symbolize? What is the relationship between the community and commodity values of water? Finally, what are the implications for the rural poor of these values and the water environment they help engender?

The evidence establishing the community value of water is of a different sort than that provided in the discussion in Chapter 2. Interviews with Hispanics and the Tohono O'odham, reported in the case studies that follow, will reveal the emotional ties these people have to water. As for the broader society, scholarly literature of historic and contemporary cultures around the world disclose water's common role in community stability. Regional newspapers give more attention to water issues than to other subjects of recognized social significance. Southwestern literature contains numerous passages that portray the enduring, symbolic value of water. From these diverse sources comes a central message: water has importance to communities beyond its utilitarian value.

The Organizing Importance of Water

From earliest times the subject of water has had a special significance to the residents of arid lands. In several passages in *The Laws*, Plato argued that of all necessities of life, water must always be subject to regulation by society because of its basic importance for human well-being and its vulnerability to people "doctoring, diverting, or intercepting the supply."[4] The Romans no less than the Greeks believed that visible water works and water institutions were of great significance to public life and to civilization itself.[5]

As settlers moved beyond the hundredth meridian into the arid American West, they discovered that establishing themselves was impossible without developing a system for allocating water. According to Elwood Mead, an early observer of western irrigation practices, until public institutions for adjudicating water disputes were developed, "there was either murder or suicide in the heart of every member" of irrigation communities.[6]

Water is no less important in the West today than it was at the time of settlement, even though the open water wars may be a thing of the past. We consulted the indexes of four important regional newspapers for the number of stories printed on water, transportation, energy, employment, and population during the period 1977–1981 (see Table 3.1). The number of articles devoted to water issues outranked those on other subjects in half of the years surveyed. (Transportation ranked second overall, followed by energy, employment, and population.) Water issues were most prominent on the pages of the *Arizona Daily Star*, followed in descending order by the *Albuquerque*

Table 3.1. Index Inventory of Regional Newspapers

Newspaper	Category	No. Articles			
		1977	1978	1979	1980
Albuquerque	Transportation	8	29	103*	48*
Journal	Energy	25	13	37	39
	Employment	24	11	15	9
	Population	1	3	4	12
	Water	34*	30*	31	39
Arizona Daily	Transportation	27	38	40	43
Star	Energy	17	6	7	9
	Employment	17	17	17	19
	Population	10	11	22	23
	Water	94*	75*	81*	95*
Salt Lake	Transportation	550	403*	506*	272
Tribune	Energy	464	232	377	372*
	Employment	65	73	52	30
	Population	13	12	27	22
	Water	817*	300	305	211
Denver Post	Transportation	68	63	650*	633*
	Energy	73	403*	521	270
	Employment	21	22	112	83
	Population	26	27	240	425
	Water	144*	65	464	515
Chicago Tribune	Transportation	667*	595*	927*	961*
	Energy	370	190	547	226
	Employment	270	245	196	315
	Population	23	61	50	115
	Water	163	124	214	170

SOURCE: Helen Ingram and Stephen P. Mumme. "Public Perceptions of Water Issues in the Four Corners States as Indicated through a Survey of Regional Newspapers: A Preliminary Report" (Paper presented at the Western Social Science Association's 25th Annual Conference, Albuquerque, New Mexico, April 27–30, 1983).
*Denotes first place rank.

Journal, the *Salt Lake Tribune,* and the *Denver Post.* The particular importance of water in the West is underscored when a comparison is made with the midwestern newspaper, the *Chicago Tribune.* In that paper only population had fewer articles among the five issues that were examined.

Its Emotional and Symbolic Importance

Water is not only more important than other resources to westerners, it is also a "different" resource with a special meaning linked to survival and security that transcends its commodity value. Many economists view such popular sentiments as misguided, and their testimony that such attitudes do in fact exist is particularly compelling. Economist Kenneth Boulding has written that public emotions and feelings associated with water are so strong that what he regards as rational solutions to water problems may never be possible.[7] In an article centered around the "water-is-different syndrome," Maurice Kelso argued that water is bound up in a number of myths such as that "water is priceless" and that water is important to the establishment of strong democratic institutions, or agrarian fundamentalism, all of which set it apart from ordinary market mechanisms.[8] In their study of six irrigation communities, Maass and Anderson concluded that water is "a special product" and that farmers generally believed it "should be removed from ordinary market transactions so that farmers can control conflict, maintain popular influence and control, and realize equity and social justice."[9]

Articles on water issues in regional newspapers further describe this emotional and symbolic significance. Phrases such as "life giving" and "precious" or stories emphasizing the importance of water to posterity or survival appeared in about one-fifth of the sample of newspapers. The type of treatment found and classified as symbolic can be illustrated in a few examples:[10]

> Drought in the West is as certain as death and taxes . . . water is fundamental.
>
> Water is our lifeblood in this state.
>
> We are allocating scarcity.

In this water-poor desert, water is life itself, if you know where to find it.

A Westerner's priorities are, in order, (1) water, (2) gold, (3) women. You may tamper with the latter two but not the first.

This substantial emotional and symbolic meaning we term the community value of water, and it is toward a more complete description of the term that we now turn.

Water and Community

Long caught up in the web of human relationships and social dependencies, water is closely tied to social organization. After all, collective decision making first developed to provide basic goods and services that individuals could not provide, or not provide so well, for themselves. Among such services are fire and police protection and water supply. Further, decisions about water have commonly been made on the basis of community rather than individual interest. Spanish colonial water law, from which much of our present western water law is derived, went to great lengths to protect the public interest and place it above parties seeking particular water rights. "The water retained by the Spanish American town was held in trust for the benefit of the entire community. It was not the property of the inhabitants of that town, either individually or collectively, but rather was the property of the collective body itself."[11]

The *acequia* system of the Hispanics in northern New Mexico, discussed further in Chapter 4, is one example of the importance of water to community. As the community developed, the farmers built, maintained, and operated the water system together. Raymond Otis created fiction from the long-standing Hispanic obligation to share in water construction, allocation, and management. According to Otis, a man can stand the loss of a wife, a field, or an arm, but not the ditch. After a bad storm, every man in the *Little Valley* grabs a shovel and restores his segment of the ditch before he even thinks of damages to his house or anything else. The *mayordomo* (ditch boss), a job that is passed around, is always obeyed, and the irrigation schedule is faithfully kept.[12]

The same sort of reciprocity or mutual trust that is basic to community life that Otis wrote about among the Hispanics also emerged among Anglo settlers. Mormon pioneers established communities on the basis of irrigation. Ralph Moody wrote of resolving water conflicts through reasonable give-and-take among homesteaders. Moody and his near neighbors at the tail of the irrigation ditch found themselves in pitched battles with farmers at the ditch head during a drought, when water seldom reached the tail, until people got together and agreed to share shortages.[13]

The saguaro harvest ceremony so central to Tohono O'odham community life was regarded as responsible for bringing the rain. The O'odham were similar to many other native peoples living in arid lands who believed that droughts were not merely acts of nature but the vengeance of the gods brought upon them by the breach of ceremony or obligation. Florence Cranell Means created a story of a three-year drought among the Hopi during which many suffer. It is only when one by one the surviving Hopi publicly confess their sins that the gods relent and a long, gentle, life-giving rain falls.[14]

Water was central to Indian culture not just for its life-giving properties but also for its role in myth. "Because the Pueblo Indians have been a people without a written language, historical fact can often change to myth; but since myth is their only window to history, the dimensions of myth itself form an autonomous reality."[15] The mythical role of water is strongly reflected in Frank Waters's *The Man Who Killed the Deer*. A Pueblo father tells his son who is about to be initiated into manhood:

> You will be taught the whole history of our people, of our tribe. How they had their last arising from the deep turquoise lake of life at the center of the world, the blue lake in whose depths gleams a tiny star, our Dawn Lake. How they emerged from a great cave whose lips dripped with water to congeal into perpetual flakes of ice white as eagle-down. You will understand, then, son, why those of our clan are called the Deep Water people: why our kiva, this kiva, is called the eagle-down kiva; the meaning of our masks, our dances, our songs. You will see this cave. You will see this lake—our Dawn Lake.[16]

The Community Value of Water

Fairness

Fairness, like water, is fundamentally important to social arrangements, and so it is not at all surprising that communities have been preoccupied with the fairness of water distribution. In Spanish colonial law governing water allocation, such relatively objective criteria as title and prior appropriation were tempered by a number of other, more subjective issues related to fairness. Judges attended to the 1720 Santa Fe guideline, "divide the waters always verifying the greatest need . . . and giving to each one that which he needs."[17] Rights of third parties that might be damaged by new upstream water uses were protected. Above all the rights of the collective community were considered. "There is no question that in Spanish and Mexican judicial systems the rights of the corporate community weighed more heavily than those of the individual."[18]

The rules of fairness in water allocation are honed to their sharpest edge in irrigation communities. In their historical study of six such communities in the United States and Spain, Maass and Anderson found that equity far outweighed efficiency as a decision rule for water allocation. In the cases they studied, unequal treatment of individuals in the same situation or category is avoided. Rotation is the common practice and on the whole is faithfully honored.[19] As Oliver LaFarge notes in *The Mother Ditch/La Acequia Madre*, a book about irrigation in northern New Mexico, a good neighbor "closes their gate on time."[20] In Valencia, the ordinances state a generous, general principle that all farmers have an obligation to give aid to those who have the greater need.[21]

Fairness is not the same thing as equality in irrigation communities. Water is distributed by rules of seniority (first in right, first in time) or proportionally by size of holding. As a rule, irrigators are more concerned with fairness in process than equality in results. The fairness of procedures is judged according to whether or not the procedures prevent control from being imposed from outside the community, or arbitrary actions from the community's officers. Above all, community members must be satisfied by their own participation in determining procedures.[22]

Participation and Local Control

The attitude that the people themselves should have a strong voice in water decisions is found among local water users throughout the world. Maass and Anderson found, in the six irrigation communities they studied, a variety of institutions and procedures that were used to resolve conflicts over water allocation. The maintenance of local participation and control was the overriding concern in settling disputes, and when institutions or procedures threatened these overriding values, they were replaced with others.[23]

The proportion and content of articles in western newspapers dealing with participation in water resources attest to its importance as a regional value. Nearly 10 percent of the articles about water referred to participation, and of these more than a quarter treated participation in symbolic and emotional terms. People react strongly if they believe their participation has been denied. In one case the apportionment of funds by the state legislature for a common water system to service two small New Mexico villages, Canjilon and Cebolla, was vigorously protested by Canjilon because its residents had not been notified of pending legislation. One resident termed the measure "a political maneuver which would rob Canjilon of water which rightfully belongs there."[24]

Scholarly literature attests to the importance of community involvement in the development of successful irrigation projects worldwide.[25] The strength of indigenous irrigation systems is that they involve the farmers in allocation of water, maintenance of the system, and establishing the rules for resolving disputes. The staying power of the *acequia* system in northern New Mexico lies to a large extent in local autonomy in management, according to local customs and traditions. Individuals are bound to the community through their participation in water matters. "Individuals identify dams and ditches by names of ancestors who through the centuries helped maintain them—thus proclaiming their inheritance through their communities. This is not done in a romanticized fashion; rather, it serves as an important community focus for personal identity."[26]

Opportunity

Prevailing western dialogue indicates that if you have water, you have a chance; if not, you are done for. Western newspapers make very clear the opportunity value of water. New Mexico State Engineer Steve Reynolds described water "as simply the limiting factor."[27] According to former Utah Governor Scott Matheson, we have little time left to take charge of the small amount of water that gives us life.[28] The unquestioned reason given for the slow death of the little New Mexico town of Colonias was loss of water when the Pecos River changed channels and left the town high and dry. "Before the Pecos began to wander, Colonias was a prosperous farming village on the main wagon road from Santa Rosa to Las Vegas. Only when it was deprived of water did the town begin to die."[29]

Water represents opportunity less because the water itself has economic value than because control over it signals social organization. A community that cannot hold on to its water probably does not have what it takes to amount to very much. Strong communities are able to hold on to their water and put it to work. In their thorough study of the relationship of water to social organization, Robert and Eva Hunt observed, "What does emerge from this material is a quite consistent picture of a strong relationship between irrigation and power."[30]

Indian peoples in the Southwest and the Hispanics in the Upper Rio Grande Valley feel that they have been denied the community values associated with water, including equity, participation, and opportunity. For Indians, failure to secure a water supply is but one more example of the dominant culture's failure to afford equity to Indian peoples. Consider the words of Wendell Chino, President of the Mescalero Apaches:

In the nineteenth century, direct force was used to take over Indian lands. The danger today is more subtle. Under the cloak of legal strategy and executive department policy decisions, a real threat is stalking all Indian leaders. These decisions regarding legal strategy and policy are designed to dry up the water from what little land is left to us. We must be alert. We must protect our rights. The consequences of losing our water would be as serious as those following the loss of our lands in the nineteenth century.[31]

Broken promises mark the trail of Indian water rights controversies. Nowhere is the gap between promise and reality more poignantly portrayed than with the Fort Belknap tribe in Montana that won the water rights lawsuit enunciating the *Winters* doctrine, which "reserved" water rights for Indians sufficient to "practice the arts of civilization." Today, the water use of the Fort Belknap Indians is about what it was at the time of the historic court decision, while the diversions of others have increased greatly because of federally financed reclamation projects not available to the Indians. The quality of life of the Indians has remained among the poorest in the nation.[32]

The Salt River Indians near Phoenix feel twice deprived of their rightful voice in water matters. First, they object to the Kent Decree of 1910, issued by a federal territorial court before Arizona became a state, which they believe unfairly limits their rights. Second, they object to the removal of their lands from the service area of the Salt River Project Water Users Association, which they regard as representing only Anglo development interests.[33]

The Hispanics in the Upper Rio Grande and the Tohono O'odham in southern Arizona whom we interviewed made it very clear that money was no substitute for the opportunity value of water. As one Indian said, "Money is just spent and the people are left with nothing. With water, there is something in the future."[34] A Hispanic replied when asked how he felt about people who sell water, "It is clear they have forgotten how their grandfathers made their living."[35]

Frank Waters writes about the association of control over water and community survival. The elders of the tribe count

2 features of AZ terrain
  water & flat open space
     both connected
  implications for life & dev
        - dev patterns - physical
           (leap frog)
        - water sources - delegation
        - env. impact - swimming
          pools
        - determines econ base
          - agri, hi tech investment in
            arizona city resort h2o rights
All these features of water
make it highly politicized
        - hist
        - fed govt
        - state govt/ region
        - local govt
        - quasi/shadow govt
          - scope of power

H2O one area where seeming consensus
exists -- need it -- but
what are implics of such
consensus? (see small
                    report)

the slipping away of the old, good ways to the loss of Dawn Lake, now under the control of the the United States Forest Service and open to Hispanic grazers and Anglo picnickers. In frustration an Indian agent shouts at the Chief: "Let us forget this thing. Why should you cause trouble to the Government? Hasn't it given you a hospital, school, a new ditch so you can have water for your fields, a threshing machine?" The old man answers patiently: "They schools, but mebbe soon no children. They hospital, but mebbe soon people they dead, no sick. They new acequia and maquina, but mebbe soon earth she die too. This Dawn Lake our church. From it come all the good things we get. The mountains, our land, Indian land. The Government promised. We no forget. This we say."[36]

In Anglo society, too, water is symbolic of opportunity. Farmers in Arizona have continued to support the Central Arizona Project, despite mounting evidence that project water will cost them more than they can afford to pay. From their viewpoint, it is inconceivable that gaining control over water could be a mistake, regardless of the cost.[37]

Caring for the Resource

Westerners who live close to the land are aware of water's importance in the natural environment. But even native westerners living in urban areas hold a respect for water. From water running down the street due to an overirrigated lawn to massive fountains heralding the latest residential land development, perceived waste offends people who care for an important resource.

This is not a rational choice to plug leaks and fix leaky faucets, but rather a deep feeling that waste or excess is incompatible with and even irreverent toward such a valuable and fundamental part of the environment. Spanish water law clearly recognized that a water right did not include freedom to waste. Even in the case of spring or well water originating on a piece of private property, the owner could not deprive his neighbor of its use simply by wasting that which he did not need.[38]

One non-Indian observer of the disputes over tribal claims to water, although concerned about the potential consequences for non-Indians, nevertheless privately expressed the opinion that tribes would probably make better managers of the water than the current system because of their stronger sense of stewardship. Indeed, it is likely that some of the existing excess in western water use would not have occurred had the traditional practice of leaving it in the stream until it is needed not been replaced by a "beneficial use" and "priority" system that hastened the capture of water.

Community Value, Commodity Value, and Material Improvement

The "cold-eyed" analyst may be skeptical of the utility of poor rural people pursuing the community value of water. If material improvement is sought, surely water should be treated like a material commodity instead of pursuing some mirage like "community value." Moreover, isn't it this same noneconomic viewpoint that "water is different" that fueled the "develop at any cost" passion, which stands so much in need of correction in this time of budget austerity? Community values *are* basically nonmaterial and symbolic—the human stuff about which novelists write, or the attitudinal mindsets within people to which politicians appeal. It is certainly arguable that if economic development is really the aim of the poor rural communities, water should be treated like any other commodity that can be used or sold depending on what brings the highest economic returns.

But the fact is that many, perhaps most, people do *not* feel about water the way the "cold-eyed" analyst suggests that they should. In economically developed communities, this emotional relationship to water has become obscured because the smooth running of institutions that secure water is taken for granted; water is as easy as turning on a faucet. Even in these communities, however, when control over water is threatened, the strength of the tie reemerges. When the United States District Court struck down New Mexico's antiexport statute allowing El Paso access to groundwater supplies in New Mexico, citizens of the state reacted angrily. The *Albuquerque Journal*'s editorial was, if anything, understated: "Quite simply New Mexico's border has been breached. Theoretically, outside municipalities or states—or anybody—can now apply to claim every unappropriated drop of New Mexico water. It is ironic because New Mexico has carefully guarded and conserved its water resources, only to lose a lawsuit to a city and state that takes far less care of the resource."[39]

Since the community value of water is a common thread among a variety of cultures, both developed and undeveloped, it is reasonable to suggest that the community and commodity value of water need not be incompatible, but may instead work together. Indeed, both the stewardship component of water's community value and the marketplace value of the water commodity signal the need for increased care in its use under conditions of scarcity.

The lessons from the literature on international development projects are also relevant.[40] They teach that the process of development occurs in stages. In the earliest stage, which is difficult but essential, the goal of efficiency takes a backseat to other objectives, such as engaging the participation and commitment of community leaders and members. Once community capacity to act effectively has been developed, attention can shift to efficiency. Because of the close emotional ties of water to community, some international development experts have recommended rural water projects as a means for building community capacity.[41]

The community value of water should be regarded as the broad context within which economic values may be pursued. Unless community values of water are satisfied, debilitating attitudes of hopelessness persist, fostered by perceptions of injustice, lack of efficacy, and loss of opportunity. Rather than being inimical to economic progress, their fulfillment seems to be a necessary condition for that progress. Moreover, the acquisition of secure control of water through a community's own initiative and effort may supply the key ingredients of participation and belief in the possibilities of the future that are essential to sustained economic improvement.

The Challenge for the Rural Poor

Whether or not the rural poor can fashion a water resource strategy that is responsive to community values and also provides economic benefits will be determined in particular concrete cases. Although community and economic values are compatible in the abstract, in the real world the strong assertion of the commodity view of water by the dominant Anglo culture presents a formidable challenge to particular poor communities. Before we turn to the cases of rural Hispanic and Indian water conflicts, some lessons can be drawn from the general discussion of the commodity and community perspectives on water presented in this and the previous chapters.

1. Water ownership is unlikely to produce a collective windfall affluence for either tribal or Hispanic communities. Market prices for rights will increase and some individual rightholders may profit handsomely, but in most instances the holdings are either too small or the community population too large to support an "oil sheikh" strategy, even if the political process would tolerate such an approach. There may be local areas in which the development of major commercial or industrial enterprises such as ski resorts or power plants dramatically increase the price of water rights, but no general strategy should be built on the assumption that sizable economic gains can be achieved simply by holding rights and waiting.

A second, and more important, reason for discarding this strategy flows from the community value discussion just concluded. Unless the cultural and community base is secure, any strategy for economic gain through the sale or lease of water rights is likely to be met with hostility.

2. Low-valued or economically marginal uses of water will be put under increasing pressure practically everywhere, even though dramatic increases in market prices will occur only in some localities. For tribes this means that it will be increasingly difficult to gain control of water that is already fully appropriated, particularly if the proposed uses of that water are low-

valued economically. Resistance against Indian control over water may be softened if Indians agree to lease back their water to existing or other users, at least for a period of transition. Yet for different reasons, tribal leasing itself is sometimes opposed. However, in a water-scarce environment such as the Southwest, it is likely that some enterprising municipalities or businesses will be interested in leasing Indian water.

Hispanics in the Upper Rio Grande are seeing water rights in their communities being bid away acre by acre. Although the process is not fast paced or substantial at this point, it can be expected to increase over time. Particularly vulnerable, since they produce relatively few dollars per acre-foot of water applied, are the alfalfa and forage crop uses of water, which predominate in most Hispanic communities. In the continuing shift of water from irrigated agriculture described above, it is the water rights associated with these crops that are most likely to be the target of prospective buyers.

The production of economically more valuable crops is more sustainable. Again, it is a question of degree. Recall that relatively little irrigation water can go a long way in meeting municipal and industrial needs. Despite the extent of regional growth, quantitatively there does not have to be wholesale reduction in irrigated agriculture to meet the water needs of this growth.[42] In the marketplace, other things being equal, water from lower-valued crops can be obtained more cheaply than water from such crops as vegetables and fruits.

3. The protection provided to existing and prospective Indian and Hispanic water users by legal institutions is threatened. This conclusion refers back to the theme introduced early in Chapter 1. Fundamental institutional and policy change is occurring in western water. The economic scrutiny recently applied to Indian water claims, as described in Chapter 2, is illustrative. Similarly, the Rio Grande Compact that divides the United States' share of that river among Colorado, New Mexico, and Texas has effectively insulated Hispanic water rights in the upper basin region from water demand in Santa Fe, Albuquerque, or even El Paso.[43] Yet with the challenges

to compacts that are occurring as a result of the *Sporhase* decision, this protection should no longer be considered absolutely secure. Old rules and habits cannot be considered as fixed. Instead the newly emerging institutions, policies, and patterns must be discerned and learned. It is an "old saw" that such times breed opportunity for the wary and danger for the unwary.

4. Hispanics and Indians must be actively involved in water politics if their water strategies are to be successful. With both the marketplace and the judiciary promoting the commodity value and view of water, Indians and Hispanics must assert their community values politically through elective and agency processes. Further, political and governmental arenas will cast the new rules for the water management era to come.

There are apparent disadvantages to a political strategy. The rural poor were not effectively included in the political arena when coalitions were formed to promote previous water development. Why should they expect to have any greater success at this juncture? Further, water politics is currently in disrepute because appropriations for "hometown" water projects are commonly perceived to be one of the most flagrant abuses of pork-barrel, distributive politics.

Nevertheless, the political strategy offers the best hope. Chances of succeeding can be improved by acquisition of relevant education, training, and experience. The art of succeeding in politics can be learned just as the arts of succeeding in the marketplace or the courtroom. Indian success in the latter arena over recent decades has come at least in part from learning just how the judicial process works. Moreover, neither Indians nor Hispanics are novices in water politics, though the general posture until recently has been more reactive than assertive.

The disreputable image of water politics stems in part from the absence of economic accountability mentioned earlier in Chapter 2. Projects have been built that simply were economically unjustified and did not enlarge the material pie but only redivided it. In a former age of affluence such political decisions may have been tolerated, but in the present era of austerity this is less likely to be the case. Therefore, the "involvement in water politics" by Indian and rural Hispanics cannot simply mean pursuit of the "water business as usual." The commodity value of water will play a strong future role, and this value must be accommodated by the poor for their water strategy to be successful.

CHAPTER 4

Hispanics in the
Upper Rio Grande

Setting

Some of the major rivers of the western United States rise in the Rocky Mountains: the legendary Colorado River and two of its main tributaries, the Gunnison and the San Juan; the South Fork of the Platte River; and the Arkansas River. In the mountains of Hinsdale County in the southern part of Colorado are the headwaters of the Rio Grande. It flows out of the southern Colorado Rockies into the San Luis Valley, where it is fed by major tributaries such as the Trinchera, the Conejos, and the Culebra. The river enters New Mexico and flows close to the Sangre de Cristo Mountains, a southern extension of the Rockies. Here, the Rio Grande is augmented by the creeks and rivers heading in the mountains of northern New Mexico: the Rio Fernando, the Rio Embudo, the Rio Santa Cruz, and others. At Espanola, New Mexico, the Rio Chama, flowing from the San Juan Mountains in northwestern New Mexico (also part of the Rockies), forms a major junction with the Rio Grande. From there the river flows south, bisecting the state of New Mexico, then forms the border between the United States and Mexico, and finally reaches the Gulf of Mexico.

European settlements in the northern reaches of the Rio Grande, the area around and above Espanola, date from 1598. During different periods the region has been under the flags of Spain, Mexico, and the United States. People of Hispanic origin are a numerical majority in many counties of the Upper Rio Grande, and the region has maintained a distinctive, picturesque, rural character. But in the midst of the scenic beauty of the mountains, valleys, and the Rio Grande itself, family

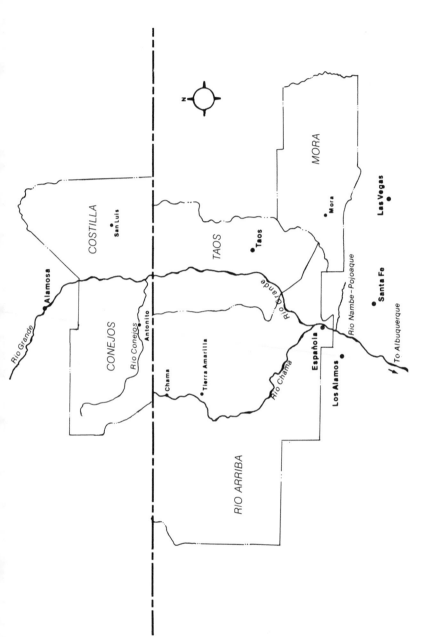

Five Counties of the Upper Rio Grande.

incomes frequently fall below government poverty levels. Feelings of lack of power over community conditions are present, sometimes pervasive. The juxtaposition of scenic enchantment and rural poverty strikes imbalanced and discordant notes.

Analysis of income statistics for southwestern states in Chapter 1 has shown the Upper Rio Grande region to be a focal point of southwestern rural poverty. There are common economic, social, and ethnic characteristics to a number of counties throughout northern New Mexico and southern Colorado, but we have for practical purposes delineated the Upper Rio Grande as a five-county area containing the counties of Rio Arriba, Taos, and Mora in New Mexico and the southern Colorado counties of Costilla and Conejos, as shown in the map. Much of Mora County, New Mexico, is not actually in the Rio Grande drainage; the county is principally in the Canadian River basin. But cultural, ethnic, and economic characteristics of Mora County link it closely to the other counties of the Upper Rio Grande, as do extended family ties. Farther north of the five-county study area, the Colorado counties of Alamosa, Rio Grande, and Saguache are also in the upper Rio Grande drainage. But the economic condition of these counties is better than that of their neighbors to the south. Moreover, these three counties do not have the heavy concentration of Hispanic people contained in the five-county area. Thus, for purposes of this case study, we have defined the Upper Rio Grande region to be the five counties identified above.

Acequias and Water Use

The five-county region is much more than a focal point of southwestern rural poverty. It is one of the oldest inhabited areas in the United States, and within it irrigation is a long-established practice.[1] The first Spanish settlement of the area occurred in 1598 at San Gabriel, across the Rio Grande from San Juan Pueblo and near the contemporary town of Espanola. The San Gabriel colony later failed, but the Spaniards founded a successful colony nearby at Santa Cruz in 1603 and firmly established the capital of the new area at the colony of Santa Fe in 1610.

The distinctive contribution of the Spanish colonists to New World irrigation practices was the *acequia*, the community ditch organization, although the Spanish explorers and colonists found the Pueblo Indians of the area already practicing irrigation and growing corn, cotton, and some other crops, and Indian irrigation practices did contribute to *acequia* development. As noted by Hutchins, the *acequia* is a fusion of Spanish and Indian traditions.[2]

The *acequias* of northern New Mexico were both a technological and organizational device. Technologically, irrigation was necessary to supplement rainfall, and so the colonists established their communities in the river valleys. The ditches that brought the streamflow to the fields commonly began at a diversion two to four miles upstream from points of use. By gravity water flows in the *acequias* along the foothills and then into the fields below. Organizationally, the *acequias* originated as associations of all persons served by the ditch and had an elected official or officials to supervise irrigation affairs. Members of the *acequia* contributed labor for repair of ditches and gates. One group wrote, "Far more than just a means of water distribution, ditch associations are the basic socio-economic unit out of which community life in rural northern New Mexico has evolved."[3] Even legally, as Hutchins has indicated, the concept of common proprietorship guided water use more than notions of individual water rights.[4]

The *acequia* tradition is not as strong in the southern Colorado counties of Costilla and Conejos as in northern New Mexico, probably because these counties were not settled until the middle of the nineteenth century. Apparently, the San Luis Valley of southern Colorado was an Indian hunting ground for buffalo and other game, and the Indians were successful in keeping non-Indians south of the valley for many years. But in 1844, Charles Beaubien, a Taos trader, obtained a large grant of land from the Mexican government covering much of present-day Costilla County. Beaubien sold some of the land in small parcels to Hispanic settlers, who founded the villages of San Luis, Colorado, and Trinchera, Colorado, in 1851 and 1852, a few years after the United States became sovereign in the Southwest. The settlers practiced irrigation in these early southern Colorado villages and brought the *acequia* tradition from northern New Mexico. Hispanic settlement of Conejos County began shortly after that of Costilla County. The Colorado territorial legislature legally recognized the *acequias*, even enacting an 1866 statute concerned specifically with "public acequias" in Costilla and Conejos counties, which attempted to enforce legal collection of assessments. Although the *acequia* tradition came from New Mexico and provided the original water institutions for the counties, subsequent Anglo settlement of the San Luis Valley introduced other governing arrangements. Eventually, the pattern of water institutions in the two counties came to be distinct from their New Mexico antecedents.

By the 1850s and 1860s, Hispanic irrigation and agricultural practices were adapting to the new U.S. legal system. By the 1860s and 1870s, perpetuation of the *acequias* under U.S. territorial law in New Mexico had been assured. By this time, also, Simmons maintains that a difference in Hispanic agriculture of the Upper Rio Grande and Middle Rio Grande had developed.[5] Small farms that averaged only ten acres in size were typical of the river valleys of northern New Mexico. But in the Rio Abajo, south of Santa Fe, larger farms were more common.

Today, in the 1980s, the *acequias* are recognized political subdivisions of each state. Although northern New Mexico and southern Colorado have changed enormously since the 1848 Treaty of Guadalupe Hidalgo ending the Mexican-American War, the importance of water for irrigated agriculture has continued. Moreover, the *acequias* have remained a vital institution in the rural Upper Rio Grande. In the 1980s, the major use of water in the Upper Rio Grande is still irrigated agriculture. Table 4.1 presents estimated water depletions, by category of use, in the three New Mexico counties for 1980. Excluding reservoir evaporation,[6] total water use is approximately 125,000 acre-feet, so that irrigation consumes about 93 percent of total depletions in the three counties.

Data are not readily available on water use in Costilla and Conejos counties, Colorado, but the pattern of water use

Table 4.1. Water Depletions by Use in Rio Arriba, Taos, and
Mora Counties, New Mexico, 1980

Use	1980 Depletions (acre-feet)
Urban	691
Rural	1,326
Irrigated agriculture	116,580
Other agriculture, livestock, and stockponds	3,464
Commercial	36
Industrial	24
Mining	1,135
Fish and wildlife	2,203
Recreation	265
Reservoir evaporation	47,334
TOTAL	173,058
TOTAL (excluding reservoir evaporation)	125,724

SOURCE: Earl F. Sorensen, *Water Use by Categories in New Mexico Counties and River Basins, and Irrigated Acreage in 1980*, New Mexico State Engineer Office, Technical Report 44 (Santa Fe, N.M., 1982).

appears similar to that in the New Mexico counties, that is, heaviest use by irrigated agriculture. We may form some approximate idea of total water use for irrigation in the Colorado counties by comparing irrigated acreage in the New Mexico and Colorado counties. Table 4.2 shows that total irrigated acreage in the three New Mexico counties was 78,520 acres in 1980. For the two Colorado counties, 1978 irrigated acreage was 162,250 acres. It is important to note that the large amounts of farm acreage reported in Conejos County combine the larger, midwestern-style farms of the northern part of that county with the heavily Hispanic area in the south. But using the total irrigated acreage of the two Colorado counties as a base implies that their water depletions are roughly twice that of the New Mexico counties, or perhaps 250,000 acre-feet per year. Thus we may estimate that water depletions in the five-county study area are about 375,000 acre-feet per year, although a portion of this use occurs in the non-Hispanic area of northern Conejos County. As a comparison, the State Engineer's office of New Mexico has estimated that total 1980 water depletion in Bernalillo County, New Mexico (the Albuquerque area), for municipal, industrial, and commercial use was 62,000 acre-feet. Thus, the rural, five-county Upper Rio Grande region has water depletions about six times as large as those of the Albuquerque, New Mexico, area.

Table 4.2. Irrigated Acres in Five-County
Upper Rio Grande

	Irrigated Acres
New Mexico[a]	
Rio Arriba	34,200
Taos	30,560
Mora	13,760
Colorado[b]	
Costilla	41,450
Conejos	120,800

SOURCES: [a]T. Clevenger and P. Carpenter, *Irrigated Acreage in New Mexico and Estimated Crop Value by County, 1980,* Agricultural Experiment Station, Research Report 498 (Las Cruces: New Mexico State University). These data are for 1980.
[b]Bureau of the Census, *1978 Census of Agriculture* (Washington, D.C.: U.S. Department of Commerce, 1979). These data are for 1978.

Agricultural Practice

As briefly described in Chapter 1, the major crops in the Upper Rio Grande are alfalfa, hay, and irrigated pasture. This pattern results, to a large degree, from the widespread ownership of cattle as the prime cash product of the region's agriculture. In two areas, however, this forage pattern is not dominant. First, in the Rio Grande and Rio Chama valleys, just north and northwest of Espanola, there is significant production of apples and other fruit, a cropping pattern especially evident around Velarde, New Mexico. Second, in Costilla County there is significant production of vegetables—for example, cabbage, spinach, and potatoes. The area around Fort Garland and Blanca, Colorado, is particularly prominent in this regard. As for cattle, the volume of the herds supported by the forage crops varies. A small farmer with four or five acres may own five head of cattle; a farmer with a somewhat larger acreage typical of Conejos County may have a herd of twenty-five to thirty animals.

There is a second key characteristic of Upper Rio Grande agriculture: it is a part-time occupation for many people. This part-time character of farming is especially evident in northern New Mexico. In almost every village—Chimayo, Cordova, Abiquiu, Penasco, Questa, Hernandez—community leaders indicate that the aim is to hold a full-time job, if possible, and to farm part-time. People from the villages hold jobs in the nearby towns and cities. They "work out of the community." "Working out" is normal practice in rural northern New Mexico particularly.

The principal reason for the part-time character of the farming appears to be the small size of the individual land holdings as described in the following quotes from two Hispanic residents of the Upper Rio Grande.

> Farming is part-time. There's nobody here who can do it full-time because they don't have the acreage.
>
> Interviewer: It's too small?
>
> The acreage is too small.
>
> Farming has become part-time. It used to be full-time. But people didn't get enough food from their farm. So they had to work out of the community.

The small plot size in turn stems at least partially from the traditional practice of *partible* inheritance, in which the land is subdivided among heirs, becoming smaller and smaller with succeeding generations.

In Conejos County typical land plots are larger than in northern New Mexico, and farming is more frequently a full-time occupation. In Costilla County the picture is somewhat mixed. Along the Culebra River in southern Costilla County, where there is a heavy Hispanic population, farming tends to be part-time. In northern Costilla County—around Fort Garland and Blanca—there is a tricultural community composed of Hispanic, Japanese-American, and Anglo people. Here farming is typically full-time.

With some important exceptions, therefore, farming among Upper Rio Grande Hispanics tends to be part-time, and the income derived is either supplemental to another main income or for subsistence when unemployed. In the New Mexico counties, "working out" is an accepted way of life. In the Colorado counties, there is more full-time farming, but there are still many smaller land plots farmed on a part-time basis. Of course, part-time farming is not a situation unique to Upper Rio Grande Hispanics. In parts of Colorado, Nebraska, and Kansas, for example, there is also significant part-time farming among Anglo farmers.

The jobs held outside the community, if the individual is not unemployed, vary, of course, with the location of the community. The two places of employment most frequently cited were Los Alamos National Laboratory (and its associated Zia Corporation) and the molybdenum mine near Questa, New Mexico. Many people in the southern part of the study area work at Los Alamos and typically do custodial or technical work. In Taos County, especially around and north of the town of Taos, many people hold full-time jobs in the molybdenum mine. Other important employers in the study area include the following:

offices in Santa Fe, which provide jobs for people in the southern part of the study area

the U.S. Forest Service, which provides both temporary and permanent jobs

public schools in the area, in which many jobs involve custodial work or driving school buses

the state highway department, which provides seasonal jobs

ski valleys in the study region

the perlite mine owned by Grafco Corporation between Tres Piedras, New Mexico, and Antonito, Colorado

sawmills and logging contractors in the area

It is important to note that jobs are usually difficult to obtain in the area, as reflected in the unemployment statistics in Chapter 1. More people would be interested in working full-time, but there are very few jobs available.

"We Want to Maintain Our Culture"

Irrigated agriculture serves as a supplement or subsistence to many who are unemployed or work part-time and as full-time employment to some, and therefore in an objective economic sense, water provides a floor for survival and a margin above it to many who are otherwise "just getting by." These are important functions in their own right, but to narrowly view water only as part of "the safety net" would mask the qualitative, subjective importance of water in the area. A drive through the Upper Rio Grande is sufficient to confirm that villages such as Truchas, Penasco, Chacon, Valdez, San Luis, and Conejos were historically constructed around creeks and rivers—the stream that serves the bordering farmlands is almost always the major topographic feature of these villages. In a survey of community leaders in the Upper Rio Grande, described in Chapter 6 below, many people mentioned the importance of water in their villages. One person told us, "Water is the lifeblood of our community." Another person expressed the matter by saying, "Water is part of living and part of the way we make a living. Water rights are sacred." The subjective and symbolic importance of water, sometimes obscured by numbers about water use, is clearly part of the Upper Rio Grande human environment.

Although the Hispanic people of the Upper Rio Grande have experiences of economic hardship and inadequate control over their condition, they remain a dignified and proud people. Spoken and written Spanish flourishes in the towns and villages; study of the roots of Hispanic-American culture has intensified during the last decade; and maintenance of traditions and infrastructure, such as the ditch organizations, remains highly important even though some *acequias* have languished as the result of out-migration of the young and other reasons. Indeed, to understand Hispanic society of the Upper Rio Grande one must comprehend the strong desire to retain the vitality of Hispanic culture. In the words of one of the people of the area, "We want to maintain our culture."

This desire "to maintain the culture"—often referred to as

preservationist sentiment—appears frequently in literature about Hispanics in the region and also in conversations with individuals from Upper Rio Grande Hispanic communities.[7] Although it is not our intent to enter into a protracted discussion of just what is encompassed by this phrase, particularly the term "culture," it is important to provide sufficient description to give some concreteness. At a minimum we can identify four facets of Upper Rio Grande Hispanic culture for which there is strong preservationist sentiment.

1. Language. As noted earlier, Spanish flourishes in the communities of the region. It is not simply a tradition that is clung to, it is the basic medium of everyday discourse. Whereas children of Hispanic families in Albuquerque or Denver may seek to "learn" the language in high school, children of Hispanic families in any of the numerous villages of the region learn Spanish first. Indeed, many may have to "learn" English if they want to compete in the larger society outside the region.

2. Family relationships. Whether it is expressed through deference to the older members of the family or through concern about the young person who must migrate from the community to find a job elsewhere, Hispanics place great value on the strength of family relationships. Thus, if community survival is brought into question, so too is the wholeness of the extended family threatened.

3. Attachment to the land. There is no other single subject that has engendered more conflict in the Upper Rio Grande than land. Battles over land, particularly land grants, have flared into violence on a number of occasions in the past[8] and likely will continue to occur into the future. Localized conflicts with "outsiders" over land issues occur frequently; attachment to the land is fierce. If the land base of communities were lost, it is likely that there would be no community.

4. Attachment to water. For many Hispanics in the region water is inseparable from the land. Although state law may allow water rights to be sold away from the land, to many people in the Upper Rio Grande this practice is unnatural and should be reversed. And in a practical sense, water is a string that, if pulled, will unravel the whole garment. Without water, there

there is no irrigation. Without irrigation the land will be lost. Without the land base the family will disintegrate, and without the families the community, too, will die. Without the family and the community, the language will be lost. Thus is it any wonder that to preserve their cultural heritage Hispanics seek to protect their water? Once lost, the culture almost certainly could never be regained.

The next four chapters will elaborate on this theme and explore possibilities by which water may serve as a vehicle for improving the general welfare of Upper Rio Grande Hispanics in a manner consistent with maintenance of their culture.

CHAPTER 5

San Juan–Chama, *Aamodt,* and the Importance of Water to Traditional Hispanics

San Juan–Chama

The importance of water to Hispanic culture is revealed by three major water conflicts in the Upper Rio Grande over the past two decades. All three conflicts originated in efforts by the state of New Mexico to capture its share of Colorado River water under the terms of the 1948 Upper Colorado River Basin Compact. The object of these efforts, the San Juan–Chama Diversion Project, was pursued vigorously by both federal and state officials, and the project seemingly contained something for everyone. Yet many traditional Hispanics came to view it not only as void of benefits to them but also as a direct assault upon their traditions.

Under the terms of the 1948 compact, the state of New Mexico was authorized 11.25 percent of the Upper Basin water.[1] Down-scaling earlier optimistic estimates of 7.5 million acre-feet annually available to the Upper Basin to a more conservative 5.8 million total acre-feet left New Mexico with a federally estimated, annual average allocation of 647,000 acre-feet of water.[2] Given rapidly expanding uses of water from the lower Colorado River Basin, New Mexico sought ways to put this limited entitlement to use and thereby secure it for the future.[3]

Since much of New Mexico's existing agriculture and projected population lay in the Rio Grande Basin instead of the Colorado, part of the solution chosen was an interbasin diversion of Colorado River water for use in the Rio Grande just east across the Continental Divide. As conceived, the San Juan–Chama Diversion Project would tunnel water from tributaries to the San Juan River, itself tributary to the Colorado, into the Chama River, a tributary of the Rio Grande. Initially, sponsors tried unsuccessfully to have the bill included in the 1956 Colorado River Storage Act. They were subsequently successful, however, in tying the project to authorizing legislation for the Navajo Indian Irrigation Project approved June 13, 1962.[4]

The San Juan–Chama legislation was popular, as it appeared to provide broadly distributed benefits. The project would be underwritten by the federal government. It would enable New Mexico to claim a substantial part of its state entitlement to the Colorado with the Bureau of Reclamation planning for total diversions of 110,000 acre-feet of water annually. The major beneficiaries included the city of Albuquerque, eventually apportioned 48,000 acre-feet; four proposed northern New Mexico irrigation units (Llano, Pojoaque, Taos, and Cerro), together apportioned 39,000 acre-feet; and the Middle Rio Grande Conservancy District (MRGCD), allotted 20,900 acre-feet. There were also lesser urban and irrigation uses and allowances for evaporation.[5]

The San Juan–Chama legislation was initially backed by practically everyone in New Mexico. City officials in Albuquerque strongly backed the legislation, and agricultural interests associated with the MRGCD in central New Mexico were staunch supporters. Moreover, there can be little doubt that initially the legislation was also endorsed by northern New Mexico Hispanic leaders. Hearings on the legislation were held on July 9–10, 1958; May 20, 1960; March 15, 1961; and April 24–26 and June 1, 1961.[6] Northern New Mexico agricultural interests were represented by Pablo Roybal of Nambe, New Mexico, Filiberto Maestas of the Santa Cruz Irrigation District near Espanola, New Mexico, and Bill Cater and Andres Martinez of the Taos area. Review of the committee hearings does reveal some initial notes of discord. For example, in 1958 Joseph Montoya, then U.S. House of Representatives member from New Mexico, stated:

> If the committee will permit me, I would like to suggest a specific declaration on the part of the committee indicating that the existing water rights that appertain to the landowners in the Questa and

Cerro, New Mexico part of the project be fully respected in the final planning of this project. This assurance has been given to me by responsible officials of the State of New Mexico who have been working in cooperation with the Bureau of Reclamation on this project.[7]

The Cerro project was later cancelled by the Bureau of Reclamation on the basis of geological infeasibility. But this statement by Montoya and a similar comment by Senator Dennis Chavez expressed a note of concern in the Hispanic community. The committee reviewing the legislation did not make the specific declaration of intent that was requested, however, and the San Juan–Chama legislation had such strong initial support that whatever initial doubts Hispanics had were subordinated.

The Taos Projects

After passage of the San Juan–Chama legislation in 1962, coordinating councils were formed in both Taos County and Rio Arriba County to assist in planning the projects. These councils contained Hispanic agricultural representation. In Taos County the projects originally planned were the Cerro project near Questa in northern Taos County, the Rio Hondo project just north of Taos, and the Rio Grande del Rancho project south of Taos. The Cerro project and Rio Hondo project were declared geologically infeasible, but planning for the Rio Grande del Rancho project and its associated Indian Camp Dam continued. By 1971, however, many Taos area citizens had become seriously concerned about the project. Federal requirements made mandatory the creation of an irrigation district or conservancy district to assume legal obligation for payment of fees and maintenance of the project. The local coordinating council voted for the creation of a conservancy district by a margin of only one vote. As Hispanic owners of small plots in the area began to realize the implications of a conservancy district, opposition to the project crystallized. Journalist-novelist John Nichols (author of *Milagro Beanfield War*) chronicled these events:

Originally, I'm sure almost 100 percent of Taos County was in favor of Indian Camp Dam. The government was going to pay 96.5% of the construction costs of the 16 million dollar dam which was going to be built, so the government claimed, solely for the benefit of the small irrigators in the Taos Valley. And even though Taos is a relatively wet area, bisected by some half dozen rivers which often run pretty strong from ample snowmelt, nobody in his right mind, in a semi-arid state, would think to knock access to more water, or at least access to a guaranteed supply.

. . . [People] began to get uneasy when they realized they would be paying off the other 3.5% construction costs over fifty years, and would also be responsible for maintenance costs which, if the dam didn't break or something untoward didn't happen, would be about $34,000 a year. . . . Then people learned that the only way the government could build the Indian Camp Dam was by imposing a conservancy district on the most irrigable portions of the Taos Valley. And when they figured out that conservancy districts are one of the more powerful political subdivisions of the state, with enormous planning and taxing and foreclosure powers, and when it began to be clear who would control the Taos conservancy district, the fourteen major ditch systems in the area which would fall within the conservancy borders, and which up until then had been represented on a local council working with state and federal agencies to implement the Indian Camp Dam, pulled out of the pro-dam council, banded into an organization called the Tres Rios Association, and prepared to fight the dam and the conservancy district tooth and nail.[8]

The account by Nichols indicates that as more information was obtained about the project and the conservancy district, opposition began to appear.[9] As Hispanic owners of small plots received more information about project design, they began to understand its implications. The opposition to the conservancy district arose on several counts.

1. The proposed conservancy district lien would have been on all lands for fifty years. Although the district's assessments would not be large, failure to pay would probably result in foreclosure. The idea of an agency having this power was intimidating to Hispanic owners of small plots of land.

2. The fees to be assessed by the conservancy district seemed relatively small, but for Hispanic owners of small plots, these fees were significant. People owning farms of ten acres or less were not commercially oriented and might not have money to

pay fees. The possible benefits of more water seemed small compared to the fees.

3. The conservancy district would supplant existing *acequias* in the watershed, and this change would imply altering Hispanic traditions in dealing with water. Change in an institution with a history of two hundred years was an important event.

4. There were major concerns about who would have authority in the conservancy district. At that time New Mexico law provided that conservancy district board members would be appointed by district judges for six-year terms. Hispanic owners of small plots felt this procedure was undemocratic, and they feared that appointed directors would represent mainly Anglo owners of large land tracts in the watershed.

Although not a complete list, these concerns of Hispanic farmers in the Taos area do indicate the major points of dispute. Underlying all of these issues was the question of whether Hispanic concerns had been adequately incorporated into project conception and design. Was the initial Hispanic participation effective or only nominal, with inadequate information about the implications of the project? Eventually the proposed conservancy district was declared illegal by the New Mexico Supreme Court on technical grounds, and the project was abandoned. In view of this outcome, and the depth of the highly emotional controversy that preceded it, the evidence implies that Hispanic participation, at least at the grassroots level, was not effective. The promise of more water hid the true social and economic costs, particularly to the small farmers. However favorable the financial terms in a national context, they were not acceptable.

The Llano Project

The Llano project was also authorized in the 1962 San Juan–Chama legislation. As originally planned by the Bureau of Reclamation, the Llano Unit would have consisted of a diversion dam on the Rio Grande just above the small community of

Velarde, with lateral canals servicing an irrigation district extending fifteen miles below the dam. Potential beneficiaries of the project included the city of Espanola, the Santa Cruz irrigation district east of Espanola, San Juan Pueblo, Santa Clara Pueblo, and other nonirrigated lands below the proposed Velarde Dam.

Prior to passage of the San Juan–Chama legislation, there had also been support for this project among leaders in the area to be serviced. As with the Taos units, a Rio Arriba Coordinating Council was formed to assist in project design. From 1965–1976, there were more than a dozen public meetings held to discuss the Llano project. But a subsequent survey by Sue-Ellen Jacobs for the Bureau of Reclamation indicated that "the majority of the citizenry [based on 108 interview-samples from communities throughout the Valley] was not aware the Bureau of Reclamation intended to begin construction on the Llano project in mid-1976."[10] As in the case of the Taos project, public participation in the Llano project did not extend deeply into the Hispanic community and was not informed and effective participation. Once the dimensions of the project became more fully known, reaction was similar to that in the Taos area, and in fact, there was communication between the Taos and Llano opposition groups.

Through efforts led by the city of Espanola, the El Llano Conservancy District was formed in 1973 and contracted with the Bureau of Reclamation for the construction of the Velarde Dam and lateral canals that made up the Llano unit. Concerned Anglo and Hispanic citizens countered by organizing a group called *La Asociación de Comunidades Unidadas para Proteger el Río Grande (La Asociación)* to investigate the details of the project and mobilize a community response. *La Asociación* leadership included the *mayordomo*, who headed the nine *acequia* associations serving the area. Among the activities of *La Asociación* was the procurement of volunteer professional services to inform and advise the river communities on alternative courses of action. One consequence of this effort was a determination that the bureau had not fulfilled its legal obligations to conduct an Environmental Impact Statement (EIS) as required by the National Environmental Protection Act of 1969.

Jacobs characterized the entire project as one of "top down planning" that neglected the interests and participation of most of the citizens affected, particularly the subsistence Hispanic and Pueblo communities. She wrote:

> This project was not initiated by people in the communities to be impacted. It originated at a higher level where national priorities for water allocations are considered and it was transmitted to the State Engineer's Office which in turn approached the City Council of Espanola and the two Indian communities (Santa Clara Pueblo and San Juan Pueblo) through the Bureau of Indian Affairs. The City Council of Espanola agreed to form a conservancy district (water management district) in order to provide the Bureau of Reclamation with a locus for development and control of the project, although Espanola has no administrative or other authority over the communities where the primary impacts were to be felt. Espanola, via the Llano Conservancy District, was designated a controller of the main canal headgates in the plan for the dam. Not only was this top down planning (which does not meet the requirements for Bureau of Reclamation projects), it was also carried out in a manner which served the interests of a small group of urban residents while setting the stage of serious disruption of long established socio-cultural traditions at the expense of rural communities.[11]

It would be incorrect to maintain that there was no Hispanic participation during authorization and design of this project. But this participation was chiefly from a small group and tended to be reactive rather than initiatory.

The result of this community opposition to the Llano Unit was a recommendation in February 1976 by the Bureau of Reclamation to the U.S. Senate Appropriations Committee that the project be closed, and the water reserved to it reallocated. The bureau explained:

> People in the project area are extremely concerned about losing control of their own irrigation facilities. For hundreds of years the farmers have been organized under a "mayordomo" system. All the farmers who have rights to water from a particular ditch system elect their own "mayordomo," or ditch supervisor. The ditch supervisor is then responsible for distributing the water, resolving conflicts, and calling men out to maintain the diversion dam and the ditch system. . . . Concern about control of their ditch system leads naturally to another worry—concern about their water rights. They fear

that if they lose control of their diversion dams and the quantity of water diverted by them, they will soon lose their water rights. The Bureau continually pointed out that their water rights are historic and superior and that their supply of water would take precedence over any other. . . . Another common objection noted in the response was the effect the Llano Unit would have on the esthetic values of the Espanola Valley. Many people decried the dam and series of canals as being ugly. Other aesthetic objections were to the effects on the Rio Grande which would have been caused by diverting water. People were led to believe, testimony to the contrary, that the 14 mile reach of the river from the Velarde Diversion Dam to the mouth of the Rio Chama would go dry. . . .[12]

The fate of these projects illustrates the conclusion that initial participation in the San Juan–Chama project by Hispanics, especially Hispanic owners of small plots, qualitatively tended to be more superficial. As more information was obtained and actual participation was realized, strong opposition to the projects developed. The threat of the project to Hispanic traditions, especially to the *acequias*, was perceived as a major issue, and eventually the projects came to be perceived as externally imposed rather than responsive to the community needs.

Aamodt

Apart from the specific political and development issues raised by the proposed irrigation units, the desire to implement San Juan–Chama also generated the legal dynamics that led to what became known as the *Aamodt* suit.[13] Here too, the agenda was formed outside the affected communities, with profoundly divisive consequences for Pueblo and Hispanic communities in the Upper Rio Grande.

The origin of the *Aamodt* suit lay in the need to manage the apportionment of the new San Juan–Chama water that would enter the Rio Grande basin. With the prospective addition of new water to the basin, ambiguities associated with unresolved water entitlement claims, both within predominantly Hispanic communities and between Pueblo and Hispanic-Anglo water users, gave San Juan–Chama contracts a degree of uncertainty and insecurity until existing rights could be clarified. Physically, the San Juan–Chama water would be indistinguishable from the native water once it entered the Chama system. Yet its contracted destination downstream could not be guaranteed if intermediate users of native Rio Grande basin water took portions of it, expansively exercising whatever they considered their historical rights to be. Then, too, some of the diversion water was to be applied upstream from the Chama's confluence with the Rio Grande. An exchange arrangement would allow the upstream user to increase what it took from the Rio Grande itself with the diversion water replacing the depletion when it entered the Rio Grande. All in all, tracking these water accounts made some means for clarifying who owned how much of what water necessary once the commitment to San Juan–Chama was made. The standard instrument sought by the State Engineer in such instances was an adjudication decree.

Consequently, enactment of San Juan–Chama was followed by the State Engineer's *Aamodt* initiative in 1966 to adjudicate water rights in court.[14] This legal initiative paralleled the debate on development and was arguably even more divisive. Adjudication of water rights clashed with the informal and community centered customs of the *acequia* associations. Again, using the words of John Nichols in describing the Taos traditions, which are equally applicable to those *acequias* involved directly in the *Aamodt* litigation:

> For hundreds of years, Taos Chicanos ran their water systems in traditional ways: who had the right to use which water, and how much of it, and for what land, was understood, often without being written down. Lacking sophisticated surveying instruments or techniques, or even feeling a need for them in such a closely knit society, boundaries were loosely defined, often changing when a fence toppled or tree fell. Too, much confusion was added when a new government, legal system, and language was imposed on the area after the 1848 war with Mexico. And today, although the state recognizes water rights according to a priority system based upon length of continuous usage, many long-time users often lack necessary or valid (in U.S. eyes) documents to prove their priority; in other cases, water that has passed from one owner to another through verbal agreement, or tradition, has no proof at all of its existence.[15]

The result of this clash has been protracted and expensive litigation accompanied by a highly charged, emotional disruption of the Hispanic, Anglo, and Indian community in the tributary watersheds of the Rio Grande to which the *Aamodt* suit applied.

It is not necessary to describe here the legal intricacies of this complex litigation, beyond the fact that the Pueblos have sought an expanded water right based upon the extent of "practically irrigable acreage" on Pueblo lands.[16] With the Rio Grande stream system already fully appropriated, any new water rights granted to the Pueblos would inevitably and adversely impact upon established rightholders. In addition, the terms of the Rio Grande Compact effectively confine the geographic scope of the water rights dispute to the portion of the basin lying above the compact accounting point at Otowi Bridge near Los Alamos, New Mexico. Without this compact restriction, any additional rights granted to the Pueblos would likely come at the expense of more junior appropriators downstream from the major area of Hispanic *acequias*. So, the combination of the two development-related institutions, the Rio Grande Compact and San Juan–Chama, have created a community conflict among the two oldest water-using societies in the region.

Without question, the *Aamodt* case has generated more cross-cultural acrimony and social rancor than anyone in the Pojoaque Valley can remember. Typical of the attitudes reflected across the Valley are the following views of individuals affected by the dispute.

A lifelong Pojoaque resident:

> We've always had real good relations with the Indians. . . . But now when an Indian and non-Indian see each other driving along the road, they don't wave anymore. They just turn their heads. . . . People are afraid. They don't know what the Indians want. . . . There have always been friendly relations here between Indians and Spanish. But now people are scared to communicate, scared to bring the subject up because it might cause violence.[17]

Another lifelong resident, married to a Pueblo woman:

> I think that the Indians should be the first to get the water. Now this has been a good year for water and there has been plenty for everyone, but I've seen some years when there wasn't even enough for this pueblo. I just hope Congress passes some kind of bill to stop this situation before it turns into some kind of race feud. I hope they settle it by law instead of guns or fists.[18]

A Nambe woman:

> If they come to meter my well, they'll be facing the barrel of my gun.[19]

A Hispanic activist:

> It's easy to understand why neighbors that had for generations lived together side by side were now caught in a legalistic vortex that seemed to care little about intermarriage, social customs or anything else.
>
> One aspect of the case had become clearly and painfully obvious to the defendants: water that had for generations been shared among neighbors, had now become a political and economic commodity. . . . It is quite obvious that the federal government, more than anyone else, had done damage to relatives, living side by side for generations and centuries, that may take an equal amount of time to correct. It has already violated one of America's long held democratic principles . . . equal justice to all. But more than that, it has caused untold upheaval in the social relations of two peoples, two peoples that have coexisted, side by side, before the arrival of Anglo government who now presume to decide the future of a people it knows little about.[20]

A tribal official:

> The people in this valley, whether they be Indian or non-Indian, have for many years lived in harmony. Whether it be asserting one's right to this or that, I think we have always shared in the water and the other resources of the valley. I would just like to say that it's unfortunate, very unfortunate, that a lawsuit of this nature pits neighbor against neighbor.
>
> Our forefathers never argued. Your grandfather, my grandfather never argued about who's going to raise the chili, who's going to raise the corn. But it's unfortunate that because of the outside influence—people buying land in the valley—because of their tinkered political philosophies or because of the philosophies brought in from the East, the West, or the South, they are inappropriate and consequently have an impact on the tradition and culture of the valley. Right now there are hard feelings. And my friends, I think there has to be a medium that we can all live by.[21]

The Politics of *Aamodt*

The *Aamodt* case and its maze of arguments and proceedings has continued for twenty years since first initiated by the State Engineer. In that time a host of actions and reactions has occurred, provoking various tactics by both plaintiffs and defendants. In 1972 the Pueblos of San Ildefonso, Tesuque, Nambe, and Pojoaque, which were directly involved in the litigation, attracted the support of other Pueblo communities, leading to the formation of the Northern Pueblo Tributary Water Rights Association (NPTWRA). Although the Pueblos were beneficiaries of free legal assistance through the Bureau of Indian Affairs (BIA) and the Department of Justice, they became convinced that they needed independent, private counsel. In 1973 NPTWRA sought to intervene itself at least partially for that purpose. However, the intervention was denied, and it was not until the late seventies that the Pueblos secured this objective at federal expense. In 1978 the four Pueblos, together with the Department of Justice, filed a complaint in intervention claiming prior and paramount rights to irrigate 21,148 acres of potentially irrigable land, based on the Pueblo Lands Act of 1933 and application of the *Winters* doctrine criteria.[22]

The 1978 filing, together with subsequent Pueblo claims, generated considerable anxiety, not only at the state level but specifically among the non-Indian residents and water claimants of the Pojoaque basin (mainly Hispanic but also including a number of more recent Anglo residents). Until then, few of the valley's residents took the case seriously, or even knew much about it. According to the *Santa Fe New Mexican*'s Dan Herrera:

> Until the conflict between state and federal policies was introduced in court, residents of the Valley did not pay much attention to the suit. . . . Pojoaque Valley Irrigation District Chairman Eddie Ortiz said that when the suit was first filed in 1966 non-Indians welcomed the chance to define their rights against an influx of newcomers. "We thought it was a good thing. Everything would be cleared. . . ." He said letters informing residents about the progress of the suit were received without much concern or notice for 13 years.[23]

The Pueblo complaint in intervention, however, cast doubt on all previously adjudicated titles as well as those not yet settled. The restructured suit caught the non-Pueblo residents by surprise and without any real organization. Many of these people lacked the means to defend themselves. Accordingly, the non-Pueblo members of the Irrigation District united to form the Pojoaque Valley Irrigation Association (PVIA) and sought legal assistance. PVIA activists were angered that the Pueblos enjoyed federal legal financing while they were obligated to finance their defense out of pocket. Describing PVIA's plight, Chairman Ortiz commented: "Ten dollars an acre [the assessment for legal fees] doesn't sound like much these days. . . . But if you take some of these elderly people with one or two acres that they grow their dinner on, and you're talking about a lot of money. And we're just beginning."[24]

Until mid-1979, the New Mexico congressional delegation, including Congressman Manuel Lujan and Senators Pete Domenici and Harrison Schmitt, did not attempt to side with either Pueblos or non-Pueblo claimants in resolving the entitlement dispute. Generally the attitude of state and congressional leaders was supportive of the state's efforts to quantify entitlements. Under pressure from the PVIA, however, Senator Schmitt sought to reduce funding for the Pueblos' private counsels in August 1979.[25] That effort failed. In January 1980, both Domenici and Schmitt met with some five hundred members of the PVIA and were convinced that the funding problem seriously prejudiced the non-Pueblo litigants' case. They pledged to "try to ensure fairness and equity" in the lawsuit.[26] Steve Reynolds, New Mexico State Engineer, joined the campaign to limit Pueblo legal funding. Reynolds's request that either the federal or private Pueblo attorneys be removed from the case was rebuffed by the Justice Department.[27]

Failing that strategy, the state and federal representatives turned to efforts to secure legal funding for non-Pueblo defendants, approaching Northern New Mexico Legal Services Director Sam Sanchez to "consider the feasibility of assisting the defendants [non-Indians of the Pojoaque Valley] who are eligible for legal aid."[28] As eventually determined, however, legal services eligibility extended to fewer than 150 of the non-Pueblo defendants, leaving the majority dependent on their own resources.

In July 1983, Senator Domenici introduced a senate bill aimed at getting both Pueblo and non-Pueblo parties to seek arbitration of the dispute. At that point, however, seventeen years into the case, the door to arbitration was locked tight.

Even the *Albuquerque Journal* criticized Domenici's proposal as "seeking to initiate further delay in attaining a judgment in the massive *State v. Aamodt* water suit."[29] Congressman Bill Richardson subsequently introduced parallel legislation to Domenici's but also introduced legislation seeking federal funds to defray non-Pueblo defense costs.[30] In August 1983, the state's governor, Toney Anaya, proposed financing for a negotiating session between Pueblo and non-Pueblo interests in Washington, D.C.,[31] to be held under the auspices of Assistant Interior Secretary Garrey Carruthers. That offer was turned down by the Pueblos, however. In a statement prepared by Attorney Bill Schaab for the four Pueblo governors, they took the position that the suit had proceeded too far already to justify exploring alternative modes of settlement.[32] The failure of these eleventh hour explorations of alternatives prompted Senator Domenici to settle for federal funding of the non-Pueblo legal defense, introducing legislation to that effect in September 1983.[33] The legislation was eventually approved in mid-November 1983, a month after *Aamodt* went to trial in federal district court. A memorandum opinion and order was issued by the court in September 1985. Its content is variously characterized by attorneys, and at least two parties to the suit plan an appeal at this writing.

Participation, Power, and the Importance of Water

Not all Hispanics, of course, feel threatened by the *Aamodt* suit. Even the leadership survey, described in the following chapter, indicates that the opinion of community leaders tended to divide almost evenly when asked, "Will the community have difficulty keeping water rights secure?"[34] What the conflicts do reveal, however, is a strong, latent, Hispanic attachment to their water rights and water practices, which when aroused by a perceived external threat, swells up and effectively organizes against that threat. The defeat of a water project in the West, such as occurred in the cases of the Llano and Taos projects, by the very people whom the projects were purportedly to serve, is highly unusual. And the funding of both the Indian

and non-Indian litigants in the *Aamodt* case by the federal
government is equally rare if not totally without precedent in
western water litigation.

There is little doubt, as these conflicts illustrate, that traditional Hispanics can be very effective in addressing water issues
when motivated to do so. The problem revealed by all three of
these illustrations, however, is their reactive character. In each
instance, the communities were defending a cause after
policies and events had evolved to such a point that defensive
action was the only course available. Parenthetically, it should
be noted that the Pueblos also were initially in the same defensive posture.

In none of these instances was there extensive participation
by traditional, "grass-roots" Hispanics in the initial development of the policy or decision. The questions and agenda were
set by others. What power existed was for the most part a power
to prevent rather than to create or formulate. This assessment
is also buttressed by answers to questions in the survey discussed in the next chapter. Respondents were asked two questions about their community's participation and control over
policy decisions about water.

1. Do you think people in your community feel that governmental
   decisions at state and national levels satisfactorily reflect their
   interests in water matters?

2. Do most people feel that they have a voice in decisions made
   about water matters in state and national capitals?

The first question dealt with the issue of whether people felt
their interests were represented in water decisions and put
slightly more emphasis on the outcome of the political process.
The second question was about perception of power to influence
decisions and put more emphasis on the process itself.

Tables 5.1 and 5.2 indicate that respondents in the survey
felt by substantial margins that water decisions frequently did
not reflect their interests and that they did not have a voice in
many government water decisions. These answers tend to indicate a certain alienation from state and national governments.
Inadequate power over water decisions and the idea that water
policy makers do not listen to the people of the area seem to

Table 5.1. Attitudes about Government Water Decisions

"Do state and federal government water decisions satisfactorily reflect interests of people in the area?"	No. of Responses
Yes	17 (17.5%)
No	55 (56.7%)
No firm answer	25 (25.8%)
TOTAL	97

Table 5.2. Perceptions about Popular Voice in Water Decisions

"Do most people feel that they have a voice in decisions made about water matters in state and national capitals?"	No. of Responses
Yes	27 (28.1%)
No	50 (52.1%)
No firm answer	19 (19.8%)
TOTAL	96

underlie these responses as amplified by their explanatory comments. The pervasiveness of negative responses to these two questions lends credibility to the hypothesis that there is a sense of powerlessness among many Upper Rio Grande Hispanics.

A concluding note to this chapter may portend a change from the reactive posture of the past. In 1983 the congressional appropriation for the Bureau of Reclamation, as amended through the efforts of Senator Domenici, included $3 million for repair and rehabilitation of diversion structures, ditches, and headgates of nine *acequias* in the Velarde, New Mexico, area. These are the same *acequias* that successfully opposed the Llano Project. The Bureau of Reclamation had been doing design work on this project since 1977, and the appropriation had been in discussion phase since then. Total appropriation for ditch and diversion structure repair in the Velarde area could eventually be as high as $12 million over a several-year period.

CHAPTER 6

Economic Development and Hispanic Preferences for Water Use

Previous Work on Economic Development

Under the impact of the Great Depression of the 1930s, the U.S. Department of Interior and later the U.S. Soil Conservation Service undertook sociological and physiographic studies of northern New Mexico. A recent edition of some of the papers from the Tewa Basin Study of 1935 is a classic in sociological studies of the area,[1] detailing living conditions, physical facilities, and the social setting of northern New Mexico in the 1930s. At this time there was hope that with its substantial water resources, the Upper Rio Grande would become the site of projects similar to those of the Tennessee Valley Authority (TVA) in the South. Indeed, active discussion occurred in the area, and apparently in government circles, about the possibility of setting up projects similar to those in the TVA.

Another 1930s effort was the Taos Project (distinct from the 1970s project of the same name), a program begun in 1939 and ended with the onset of World War II. As described in Reid's book, *It Happened in Taos*,[2] funding for the program came from the University of New Mexico and federal government agencies, and represented a concerted effort to improve socioeconomic conditions in Taos County. As described by Reid, the project included (1) a bookmobile with motion pictures as a sidelight, (2) repair of the Acequia Madre at Cerro, a village north of Taos, (3) establishment of a soil conservation district in the Taos area, and (4) programs of hot school lunches.

During World War II and the following years, less attention was paid to the problems of the Upper Rio Grande. But interest began to build again in the late 1950s and early 1960s. A 1960 study by Burma and Williams[3] sets forth three main areas for potential economic development of northern New Mexico: (1) agriculture, (2) forest product industries, and (3) recreation-tourism. Efforts to improve educational levels in the area were also assigned high priority. In the same period, Peter van Dresser wrote about the area and portrayed the solution to rural poverty in northern New Mexico as possible through "biotechnic" development.[4] His approach avoided notions of new, large industries in favor of emphasis on cottage industry development. People would produce their own building materials through small sawmills and small brick or adobe kilns, and they would produce the area's food requirements by operating small-scale bakeries, canning operations, and related enterprises. Indigenous, handcrafted items such as furniture, woolen rugs, and shawls would become exports from the region. Van Dresser's emphasis on small-scale development in northern New Mexico anticipated the writings of E. F. Schumacher on appropriate technology.

Ferran's 1969 doctoral dissertation on the economic development of northern New Mexico focused on the need for cooperative development of agriculture and other industries in the area.[5] He described the potential for a rural development corporation that would be responsible for (1) extended education programs for adults and vocational training; (2) agricultural cooperatives for cattle management and for vegetable-fruit farming; and (3) cooperatives for production of handcrafted furniture, woven items, and jewelry. Ferran was at that time Economic Development Director of the Home Education Livelihood Program (HELP), which was a particularly important development organization in the Upper Rio Grande in the late 1960s and early 1970s and continues its service role in the 1980s. Over the years this agency has undertaken an array of projects to improve economic and social conditions in the region, funded primarily by the U.S. Office of Economic Opportunity (OEO).

Another agency formed to assist the northern counties was the North Central New Mexico Economic Development District, created by the state of New Mexico in the late 1960s. Key documents from this agency are the 1969 and the 1975 Overall

Economic Development plans (OEDP).[6] The 1969 OEDP set three priorities for northern New Mexico: (1) education and training; (2) development of physical infrastructure such as water and sewer facilities, medical facilities, and roads; and (3) improved use of area natural resources. The 1975 OEDP adopted a principal goal of improvements in community facilities such as courthouses, police and fire stations, community water and sewer facilities, and libraries. This agency is still active in northern New Mexico, although its level of effort has been reduced from the early 1970s.

In the early 1970s the Four Corners Regional Commission also sponsored a series of studies on the potential for agricultural and forestry development in the Commission's target area, which originally extended to counties in the four states. Despite the larger area of concern, the studies, undertaken by New Mexico State University, Colorado State University, and Utah State University, are quite relevant to the Upper Rio Grande itself. Some of the industries studied were vegetable production, alfalfa dehydration plants, feedlots, particleboard production, and plywood production.[7] We return to these findings below.

For the Upper Rio Grande counties in Colorado—Costilla and Conejos—the San Luis Valley Regional Development and Planning Commission and its predecessor, the San Luis Valley Council of Governments, have produced several reports concerned with economic development. The *San Luis Valley Labor Force Survey* of 1977 contains data on underemployment, seasonal work, employment by industry, and wage and salary levels in the San Luis Valley,[8] and the 1980 *San Luis Valley Overall Economic Development Program* contains summaries of economic activity in each county and discusses important natural resources in the valley.[9] The latter document also summarizes a number of potential economic development projects such as potato processing plants, tourism promotion, community sewer system improvements, and wood processing plants. The Regional Development and Planning Commission continues to be engaged in economic development activities that have potential impact on Conejos and Costilla counties.

Focusing on agriculture, Clevenger has recently identified steps that could increase agricultural economic productivity in the region.[10] He identifies inadequate marketing capacity as the chief constraint to northern New Mexico agriculture and calls for measures such as education, outside promotion, and improved sources of inputs as means of stimulating agriculture in the region. Clair Reiniger Morris and associates completed a report concerned specifically with water in northern New Mexico in 1984.[11] Their case study of Sena describes in detail one of the rural villages in northern New Mexico and the ways in which water is used in the community. The social pattern of life in Sena is minutely described and demonstrates the continuing importance of the *acequia* in contemporary Hispanic rural life.

Alternative Water Use Possibilities

Economic development possibilities for Hispanic communities are, of course, not limited to water-using industries. However, the focus of this study is on the relationship between water and poverty.

Let us suppose, for the moment, that nonagricultural water-using industries were economically feasible in the Upper Rio Grande. Using water in these activities to obtain a better return would involve transfers of water from the agricultural sector to industrial, recreational, or other enterprises. In short, water rights now belonging to Hispanic farmers would have to be sold to private firms in order to increase the return on water, as is already occurring to some extent. In other words, farmers could earn a higher return by selling water than by using it. If, for example, the net return on one acre-foot of consumptive use of water in growing alfalfa is $35 per year, and the water right can be sold for $2,000 with interest rates at 10 percent, strict economic analysis implies that the sale should occur. The farmer could take the $2,000, invest it at 10 percent, and earn an annual net return of $200, an amount that is clearly greater than the $35 per year return obtained from growing alfalfa. But would the rural Hispanic people of the Upper Rio

Grande be willing to sell their water? Are transfers of water from agricultural to recreational or other industrial uses likely to occur? On the same note, how do the Hispanic people of the Upper Rio Grande view additional nonrecreational activity?

Community Leadership Interviews

In order to obtain answers to these questions and others, some of which have already been reported above, we conducted extended interviews with ninety-eight community leaders, each of whom had some involvement in water affairs, throughout the five-county area. No strict, randomized procedure was applied to the selection of these leaders; nevertheless, the circumstantial evidence supports the general representativeness of the individuals interviewed within the universe of traditional water-users in the region. They were chosen through discussion with a number of consultant-residents, geographically distributed over the five-county area.

The interviews were conducted in the fall of 1983 in the homes of the respondent by other Hispanic residents of the same area. All of the interviewers had established relationships with at least some of the respondents they interviewed. Prior sessions had been held with the interviewers to discuss the purpose of the interviews, answer questions, and review the interview instrument.

There was a definite structure to each interview with appropriate introductory and explanatory remarks. The interviews were conducted in Spanish or English as determined by the respondent, and the interviews were taped if the respondent was agreeable to that practice, as most were.

It is important to state that the purpose of the interview was not simply to obtain a set of categorical yes-no answers to a set of questions. Instead, the community leaders were asked to explain the reasons for their answers, particularly since each was being asked to assess sentiment in his or her community on the subjects addressed, rather than simply provide personal opinion. We were seeking explanation, even illustrating stories, of the points the respondents were making. Consequently, although the interviews required a heavy investment of time, they enriched our understanding of the answers and produced comments that are quoted throughout the chapters of this case study.

Attitudes about Water Right Sales

Tables 6.1 and 6.2 contain data concerning practices and views about water right sales. The data in Table 6.1 indicate that sales of water rights have occurred in some areas of the Upper Rio Grande and not in others, based on the geographic distribution of the interviewees. Two areas reporting some sales are the neighboring vicinities of Taos and Questa, New Mexico. The molybdenum mine near Questa has been active in the

Table 6.1. Sales of Water Rights

Extent of Water Rights Sales as Perceived by Respondents	No. of Responses
Some sales were made	34 (34.7%)
No sales were made	53 (54.1%)
No sales made except when land and water sold together	6 (6.1%)
Not sure; no firm answer	5 (5.1%)
TOTAL	98

Table 6.2. Attitudes Toward Water Rights Sales

"How do people in your area feel about selling water rights?"	No. of Respondents
Opposed and don't want to sell	79 (80.6%)
Would sell if price is right; other forms of approval	6 (6.1%)
Haven't heard of selling water rights or haven't been approached	3 (3.1%)
Not sure; no firm answer	10 (10.2%)
TOTAL	98

water market; and companies involved in the construction of summer resort homes have expressed interest in purchasing rights in the Taos area. The overall picture is that some transactions in water rights are occurring in the Upper Rio Grande, but these transfers are more frequently occurring near larger towns than in strictly rural areas.[12]

The overwhelming response of rural Hispanics to these sales can be captured in a few quotations from our interviews: "People don't want to sell their water rights"; "People in my area are opposed to selling the water and the land"; and "Water is the lifeblood of the community, and they're not going to sell it." Table 6.2 indicates that over 80 percent of the interview respondents said that people in their community were opposed to water right sales.

The opposition to water right sales is rooted in social and cultural concerns rather than economics. The Hispanic resident quoted in Chapter 4 stated, "I don't think that the native people want to sell their land or their water rights. . . . We want to maintain our culture." This goal of cultural preservation was voiced by other rural Hispanics. Others asserted a desire to preserve a rural way of life, a sentiment not sharply distinct from the idea of cultural preservation. The maintenance of a pastoral environment with "rural peace and quiet" was one individual's characterization, and one respondent said: "We know that water is part of life and part of the way we make a living. I don't think people will want to sell their water rights."

There was no evidence that people were making calculations of expected economic gains and losses from water right sales, thereby retaining water rights for speculative future financial gain. Instead, they thought in terms of preservation of Hispanic culture, preservation of rural life, and related values. The overwhelming community sentiment against water right sales will not prohibit some sales from occurring. But community opposition to water sales forms a central element of the general social context that will govern how water will be put to use in the future.

Respondents were also asked a question about community opinion on water right leasing. Table 6.3 tabulates responses

Table 6.3. Attitude Toward Leasing Water Rights

Opinion about Water Right Leasing	No. of Responses
Don't want to lease water rights	43 (43.9%)
Probably willing to lease; other forms of approval	14 (14.3%)
Leasing would be better than selling	14 (14.3%)
Don't know; no firm response	27 (27.5%)
TOTAL	98

to this question. To some respondents the idea of leasing water was new, and there were quite a number of people who either said that they weren't sure how their community would view this idea or who did not give a firm answer. But prevailing sentiment in the survey was that Upper Rio Grande Hispanics are against leasing water. In all likelihood it is the same social and cultural factors underlying opposition to sales of water rights that also creates opposition to water leasing.

Two other questions about water rights sales probed more directly the hypothesis that people in the study area could be holding water rights in anticipation of future significant increases in prices of these rights. If this theory were correct, people would be expected to be informed about prices at which water rights sell and to have refused at least some offers to purchase water. Table 6.4 indicates that most people in the area have no information about water right prices and that, for the most part, there have not been large numbers of offers to purchase water rights that have been refused (Table 6.5).

Table 6.4. Information about Water Right Prices

"Do you have any information about prices that water rights would sell for in your area?"	No. of Respondents
Yes	20 (20.4%)
No	67 (68.4%)
Unclear; no firm response	11 (11.2%)
TOTAL	98

Table 6.5. Offers to Purchase Water Rights

"In the last five to six years, have any people had offers to purchase their water rights that they've refused?"	No. of Responses
Yes	26 (26.5%)
No	57 (58.2%)
Don't know; no firm answer	15 (15.3%)
TOTAL	98

Based on these responses to survey questions, we have rejected any hypothesis that people in the study area might be holding water rights in anticipation of future increases in water sales prices.

Questioned about information on water right prices, a few people cited specific numbers. The most interesting aspect of these responses was that the range of prices cited was very large:

Espanola area: three hundred to four thousand dollars per acre-foot[13]

Western Rio Arriba County (Chama to Abiquiu, New Mexico): fifteen to two thousand dollars per acre-foot

Conejos County, Colorado: one hundred to three thousand dollars per acre-foot

Such wide variations probably indicate poor information as well as lack of interest in obtaining more precise figures.

The major conclusion from the questions about selling and leasing water is that most Upper Rio Grande Hispanics are not interested in selling water to higher-valued uses such as industrial or recreational purposes. Some sales will probably occur in the future just as some have occurred in the past, but the community places a negative value, a discouraging value, on the limited sales that have occurred.

Views on Alternative Uses of Water

Given that sales and leases are not favored, how do Upper Rio Grande Hispanics view some specific alternative uses of water? And, how do they view various possibilities for improving economic conditions? For specificity we formulated questions about three alternative economic possibilities—truck farming, recreational activity, and forest products industries. Respondents were asked about each of these alternatives.

1. Vegetable farming. People were asked whether vegetables, such as carrots, onions, and beets, were grown in their area. Most respondents answered that there were vegetables presently grown, but we must interpret these answers carefully. In northern New Mexico many people have gardens as part of their small farms, and vegetables are grown for home use. A few farmers in northern New Mexico grow vegetables commercially, and these are usually marketed in growers' or farmers' markets—occasional markets in Espanola, Taos, and Santa Fe. Sometimes vegetables in northern New Mexico are marketed in roadside stands. But mainly vegetables are grown for home use.

The two Colorado counties present a contrast in vegetable growing. In Conejos county, most people responded that vegetables were not grown, as shown in Table 6.6. Respondents in Conejos County usually interpreted the question in terms of commercial vegetable growing because commercial farming is practiced elsewhere in the San Luis Valley. Although some farms in Conejos County have small gardens, there is little commercial production of vegetables. In Costilla County we have already

Table 6.6. Vegetable Growing in Conejos County, Colorado

"Do people in your area grow vegetables?"	No. of Responses
Yes	4 (20.0%)
No	14 (70.0%)
No firm answer	2 (10.0%)
TOTAL	20

mentioned that there is significant vegetable production, especially in the Fort Garland and Blanca areas.

2. Water-related recreation. The main water-related recreational activity that might be feasible for the study area is sport fishing. Past proposals have included the preservation of specific reaches of streams for fishing and the construction of lodges and cabins for summer fisherman. [14] The question about this activity was phrased in terms of fishing cabin and fishing lodge development, and Table 6.7 demonstrates that Hispanics in the Upper Rio Grande responded negatively to this question.

Table 6.7. Attitudes Toward Development of Water-Related Recreation

"Do people in your area want additional recreational development for visitors and tourists?"	No. of Responses
Yes	28 (28.9%)
No	54 (55.7%)
No firm answer & unclear	15 (15.4%)
TOTAL	97

Of those respondents giving firm "yes" or "no" answers, two-thirds said that their community would not want these recreational developments. The reasons for the negative attitude were many, but a principal one was opposition to the influx of outsiders. One respondent sketched his view of "the 'ugly' tourist—loud, demanding, not sensitive to the traditions, ideas, ways of people, polluting." The "ugly tourist" image is strong in the minds of many Upper Rio Grande Hispanics, and a negative view of additional recreational and tourist-related activities is frequently related to this perception.

Two qualifications are needed in interpreting these responses about water-related recreation. The first occurs in Costilla County, Colorado, an area in which there are many mountain creeks—a prime sport-fishing location—that are privately owned by large ranches in the county. People felt that the decision about sport-fishing activity would be in the hands of these private ranchers and wouldn't have much effect on the Hispanic people of the county. Second, in Conejos County, Colorado, we found a favorable view toward the development of water-related recreation. Only five of twenty respondents said people would not want it; another five respondents had no firm opinion; and ten respondents felt the community would favor this activity. Based on comments in the interviews, this favorable view of additional recreation activity in Conejos County seemed to be related to an absence of most other forms of economic opportunity.

With the exception of somewhat favorable views in Conejos County, therefore, Upper Rio Grande Hispanics tend to have negative opinions of additional water-related recreation development, though not unanimously so.

3. Forest products. Our review of the literature on economic development in the Upper Rio Grande indicated that forest product industries were often considered to be economic development possiblities within Upper Rio Grande communities, and so we asked about views of this sector. Table 6.8 reveals

Table 6.8. Attitudes Toward Forest Product Industries

"Do you think that additional forest products and wood products are possible for your area?"	No. of Responses
Yes	50 (51.6%)
No	27 (27.8%)
Maybe, perhaps	7 (7.2%)
Don't know; unclear	13 (13.4%)
TOTAL	97

that the majority of respondents felt that additional forest product industries would be possible in their area, though a significant number of respondents felt otherwise. Reasons for negative responses included the following:

1. Some respondents lived in areas such as lowland valleys where timber was not readily available.
2. Some respondents thought that area logging contracts might now be taking the maximum feasible cut.

3. Some respondents wanted to leave the forests as they are.
4. Some respondents felt that additional forest product industries wouldn't benefit the people who really needed money.

Discussion of this industry did not evoke the negative responses that came from questions about recreational activity. Moreover, as we shall see below, people tended to rate forest product industries somewhat favorably in discussing their preferences. It is reasonable to conclude that Upper Rio Grande Hispanics have some reservations about additional forest product industries, but the overall attitude tends to be mildly favorable to their feasibility and desirability. One historical explanation for this favorable viewpoint may be the fact that until the early 1960s, many small family-owned sawmills still existed in and around many villages.

To further clarify community preferences about water use and economic alternatives, we asked respondents to consider the three alternatives together (vegetable farming, recreation activity, and forest product industries) and to rank them according to the perceived preferences of their own community. Some people would only say what they felt ranked first, but the aggregate of rankings shown in Table 6.9 indicates a preference for vegetable farming. Forest product industries ranked second, and as might be expected from the above discussion, recreational activity ranked a distant third.

Table 6.9. Rankings of Alternative Economic Activities

"Would you rank these three alternatives according to what you think the preferences of the community would be?"[a]	Vegetable Farming	Recreation	Forest Products
1st	52	6	37
2d	16	25	21
3d	13	40	19
TOTAL	81	71	77

[a]Some respondents wished to rank only one or two activities. Also the actual question identified the three alternatives once again.

Before concluding that traditional Hispanics in the five-county area prefer vegetable farming and other forms of agricultural redevelopment as the main vehicle for improving economic opportunity, it is necessary to mention, first, that individuals who ranked this alternative first would frequently mention that vegetable farming might have to be supplemented by holding jobs in the present system. Especially in northern New Mexico, there was a strong sense that people would need to continue to work at other jobs. Second, in Conejos County, Colorado, the preference was for forest product industries. In this county, the predominant sentiment was that problems with water availability prevent alfalfa and hay acreage from being transferred to vegetables or other agricultural crops. Throughout the entire region, but particularly in the Colorado counties,[15] lack of water storage is a continuing problem. Its effect would be more damaging to vegetables in which an entire crop could be lost due to the absence of water in the latter parts of the growing season. For alfalfa, on the other hand, perhaps one cutting is lost. Nonetheless, the prevailing opinion in the Upper Rio Grande favors vegetable farming and other agricultural redevelopment, which are seen as most consistent with cultural preservation and rural preservation.

CHAPTER 7

Possibilities for
Upper Rio Grande Agriculture

Focusing upon Agriculture

Although economic analyses of the three possible development strategies for the Upper Rio Grande (vegetable farming, forest product industries, and water-based recreation) continue to indicate significant practical possibilities for each of these industries, in the present discussion we focus exclusively upon agriculture, the alternative preferred by the resident Hispanics. The discussion is slightly more technical than what has gone before, but its problems and prospects cannot be understood otherwise.

In previous chapters it has been pointed out that the dominant feature of water use in the Upper Rio Grande is the importance of irrigated agriculture. Moreover, we have indicated that the main features of the rural Hispanic economy are (1) primary reliance on alfalfa and irrigated pasture as crops; (2) maintenance of small herds of cattle and sheep that rely on alfalfa and pasture; (3) the importance of small plots of irrigated land, with most farms having fewer than twenty acres of land and many having less than ten acres; and (4) the importance of part-time farming, with owners of moderately small plots holding full-time or part-time jobs in towns and villages of the area. Moreover, as discussed in the previous chapter, Hispanic people of the upper Rio Grande prefer a water and economic development pattern centered around agriculture.

In addressing this preference, no attempt will be made here to develop a definitive agricultural program for the region. Yet by building on the work of others, it is possible to sketch the broad outline of an agricultural strategy as well as identify some of the problems associated with it. In general, the objective is to improve the economic return to water used in agriculture in a manner consistent with the cultural preservation imperatives of Hispanics in the region. Two elements of a possible strategy can be identified:

1. a gradual and incremental shift of some irrigated acreage from alfalfa-hay into more valuable vegetables and fruits, and
2. an upgrading and redevelopment of the northern New Mexico livestock economy.

A Gradual Shift to Fruits and Vegetables

The first element involves the greatest degree of change in existing practice, even though fruit and vegetable farming—truck crops—has a significant current, as well as historical, presence in the region. Yet, as Clevenger and Carpenter[1] point out, the gross receipts per acre for vegetables and fruits is substantially higher than the results from the existing alfalfa-pasture pattern of water use in the Upper Rio Grande.

In northern Costilla County, Colorado, a group of Japanese-American farmers has had marked success and relatively high returns growing vegetables at altitudes of 8,000 feet. This group grows carrots, cabbage, and more hardy vegetables such as spinach, cauliflower, and peas. Their success demonstrates the feasibility of specialty crops, and their high returns, even with a relatively short growing season. Of course, in the lower altitudes near Espanola, New Mexico, apples, peaches, lettuce, and even commercial flowers are candidates for a high-value agriculture.

There are numerous reports about agriculture in the study region that have asserted this proposition that some shift to vegetable and fruit farming should be beneficial.[2] It is, moreover, a shift[3] that would be consistent with the desire of Hispanic people in the region to maintain an agrarian base. There are, however, some important problems in making this transition, and brief discussion of some of these problems will reveal both the difficulty and the promise of agricultural development.

Problems with Specialty Crops in the Upper Rio Grande

MARKETING PROBLEMS

One of the main problems with growing additional fruits and vegetables in the Upper Rio Grande is the marketing of produce. In a 1983 paper, Clevenger focused on marketing as the key problem of Upper Rio Grande agriculture.[4] The difficulty can be illustrated by a description of the present marketing of Upper Rio Grande apples.

Apples are currently the main specialty crop grown in the region, and the main apple districts are in the river valleys of the Espanola area. The main markets for these apples at present are roadside fruit stands, the El Paso, Texas, vicinity, and weekend growers' markets in Espanola and Santa Fe. Apples are marketed in the El Paso area because grading, sorting, and quality requirements are low, as many of the apples trucked to El Paso find their way into the Juarez, Mexico, area.

Discussion with two major fruit buyers in the Albuquerque market (a major wholesale produce company and a major retail chain grocery) indicated that their purchases of Upper Rio Grande apples were small because sorting, packaging, and quality control problems frequently occurred with sources in this region. Moreover, both these buyers preferred to purchase fruit on a large-volume basis and suggested that Upper Rio Grande apple growers needed a marketing association for volume selling. Both large buyers stated that onions, carrots, cucumbers, and peppers could be produced in the Upper Rio Grande and sold in the Albuquerque market if grading, sorting, and packaging requirements were met.

There are a number of ways in which these marketing problems could be overcome. Expansion of weekend growers' markets in Espanola, Santa Fe, and Los Alamos is one step. Establishment of a marketing association or cooperative would provide a means of addressing the problems of grading, sorting, packaging, and volume. It is important to note that the Japanese-American farmers in the San Luis Valley have successfully resolved some of these marketing issues, and they

should not be viewed as insurmountable for other Upper Rio
Grande growers.

PROBLEMS OF RISK

Evidence has been cited that growing vegetables and fruits
would yield a high return to Upper Rio Grande farmers, but
the risks involved with specialty crops are also higher than
experienced with alfalfa and hay.

1. The market for a high-value crop may collapse. In an al-
falfa-cattle economy, the beef market may deteriorate, but cattle
can be kept until the market improves. With vegetables, this
holding action is less feasible. For example, in the fall of 1983
some Las Cruces, New Mexico, onion farmers had to plow under
their onion crop due to weak markets.

2. Actions to minimize risk are more difficult for farmers
with five to twenty acres than for those with fifty to two hundred
acres or more. The largest farms can diversify crops, and if the
market for one crop collapses, the farmer still has other crops to
market. For owners of the typically small plots of the Upper Rio
Grande, diversification would be very difficult or impossible.

3. Another aspect of risk with vegetables and fruits involves
water. In all of the five counties of the Upper Rio Grande, almost
all irrigation water is from surface water rather than groundwater, and there is inadequate surface storage as noted in Chapter
6. Almost exclusive reliance on surface water implies that crops
may not get water when needed, especially in the late summer
months. With an alfalfa stand, watering can be done in spring
and early summer, thereby obtaining at least one cutting with
a second cut feasible if water is available. But with vegetables
the entire crop will be lost if late summer water is insufficient.

Small-scale Hispanic growers may be unwilling to accept
these risks. But there are techniques through which these
risks can be significantly reduced. For example, a specialized
credit agency could provide intermediate-term, low-interest
credit to farmers to reduce dangers of market collapse. Or a

marketing association could write "forward" contracts with buyers in which some of the risk is passed to the wholesaler or retailer. Additional research could discover other means of reducing risk.

PROBLEMS WITH INPUTS: LAND, LABOR, AND CAPITAL

Another set of problems that would have to be resolved in an incremental, gradual transition to specialty crop production involves inputs of land, labor, and capital. In the preceding discussion of marketing, the importance of volume selling was mentioned. But the small land holdings of Upper Rio Grande Hispanics are not easily adapted to volume selling. Expansion of growers' markets in Espanola, Santa Fe, and Los Alamos is one approach to this problem, and the formation of associations of growers for volume selling into the Albuquerque market and other regional markets provides another.

Contemporary vegetable farming that is competitive in national markets uses significant capital inputs, particularly in the form of machinery for leveling, plowing, fertilizing, and harvesting. This capital-intensive character of modern vegetable farming implies problems for Upper Rio Grande growers since they typically do not have sufficient access to means of credit to purchase some of the machinery, and even if they did, purchase of machinery would be inefficient for most of these farmers because small, part-time farms could not use the equipment to capacity. Upper Rio Grande farmers who begin to grow vegetables and fruits will therefore not compete in national markets. They will need to rely on less capital intensive technology augmented by the possibility of a growers' association that buys the most important items of equipment and rents it to small growers. Another possibility is incremental consolidation of land holdings in which three to five farmers pool their holdings for vegetable production.

Clearly, there are important problems with even a gradual transition to more specialty crop production among Upper Rio Grande Hispanics. But these problems are potentially resolvable so that additional vegetable and fruit production in the

Upper Rio Grande can become an important part of any strategy to increase the economic return associated with agricultural water use.

Improving the Livestock Economy of the Upper Rio Grande

Traditionally, cattle and sheep have been central to Upper Rio Grande agriculture. Historically, in colonial times, the river valleys of the region were divided into plots for farming. Cattle and sheep belonging to these settlements were grazed on common lands usually ceded to the community as a whole.[5] Along with potential economic gains from a shift to higher-valued crops, there is additional potential for enhancing the economic return from the existing alfalfa-hay cropping patterns by improving and upgrading the livestock economy to which these crops are linked.

The most ambitious program that has been initiated in the last decade to redevelop Upper Rio Grande livestock is the sheep and wool program of Ganados del Valle, a community program initiated in northern Rio Arriba County in 1982 and now operating in both Rio Arriba and Taos counties.[6] The aim of the program is the redevelopment of the sheep economy of these two counties, and "redevelopment" has included devising means to obtain higher prices for sheep and using sheep to obtain more value through processing operations. Important features of the program have included (1) an upgrading of sheep stock through improved breeding practices, (2) cooperative grazing programs in which several owners of flocks pool their sheep, (3) improved marketing of sheep, and (4) the initiation of finishing operations for wool.

Significantly, a number of these program features parallel similar potential solutions to the vegetable and fruit farming strategic component.

Cattle are more important in contemporary Upper Rio Grande agriculture than sheep, but, as yet, a program for cattle, such as the Ganados del Valle program for sheep, has not emerged in the 1980s. There were efforts to improve the regional cattle economy in the 1960s and early 1970s, including intermediate and finishing feedlots sponsored by private foundations and government agencies in both Conejos County, Colorado, and San Miguel County, New Mexico. An effort to redevelop Upper Rio Grande agriculture could also include an effort to improve the existing cattle economy along similar lines to those employed by Ganados.

CHAPTER 8

Water and Opportunity in the Upper Rio Grande

Lessons from the Past and Present

The story of Hispanics and water developed in the previous four chapters reveals a number of important lessons for any effort to conceive and implement a water-based strategy for improving their welfare. First, water is widely and strongly perceived to be an essential element in the preservation of Hispanic culture in the region, and the desire to preserve that culture is of paramount concern. Whenever externally generated events such as Indian Camp Dam, Llano, or *Aamodt* threaten this cultural link to water, they engender strong community reaction. It is not that water projects are innately alien to Hispanic culture, for there was initial, enthusiastic interest in plans to bring more water to the region. Moreover, and more recently, some of the same community leaders who led the opposition to the Llano project persisted in gaining eventual federal financial support for the construction of concrete diversion structures in the Rio Grande. These diversion facilities serve many of the same *acequias* for which Llano was originally designed. The principal difference between Llano and the more recent project has been the indigenous support for the latter.

A second lesson is that Hispanics see agriculture as the economic activity most consistent with their cultural preservation objective. Although there is support for wood product industries, agriculture is the most desired water use option. Recreational uses such as sport fishing evoke actual antipathy from many, based on the expected influx of tourists into the region that it would produce. Unless and until the cultural objective is secured, there is likely to remain substantial opposition to the recreational option.

An agricultural strategy in the upper Rio Grande involves both a gradual transition to more valuable truck farming and an upgrading of the existing livestock economy. There are formidable obstacles to be overcome in making these changes and, unfortunately, the obstacles tend to be interlocking. Given these obstacles to a higher valued agriculture, is there any realistic chance for a water strategy based on agriculture to succeed in both preserving the culture and improving economic conditions? Before addressing this question, let us return to the broader context in which water decisions are made, providing more detail about the Upper Rio Grande than was supplied in our initial discussion in Chapters 2 and 3.

Compacts, Water Markets, and Public Welfare

As briefly discussed in Chapter 5, the Rio Grande Compact, which divides the American share of the river among the states of Colorado, New Mexico, and Texas, has an accounting point at Otowi Bridge between Santa Fe and Los Alamos. According to one state water official,[1] the terms of the compact effectively prevent any transfer of water rights across this institutional artifact. One result of this circumstance is that the Upper Rio Grande above Otowi, the geographical area in which most of our study region lies, is insulated institutionally from the burgeoning urban demand for water in both the Albuquerque metropolitan area and further south around Las Cruces, New Mexico, and El Paso, Texas. Consequently, the limited demand for transfer of water away from irrigated agriculture that has occurred in the Upper Rio Grande has emanated from within the region itself, largely from municipalities and industry. Since the overall economic and population growth of the region has not been large, the number of water right transfers has been small, though they have occurred, sometimes producing localized conflict.

Under these circumstances the Hispanic concern about the threat to their culture arising from the loss of water from irrigated agriculture might appear overblown. However, there are at least two major arguments otherwise, one retrospective and the other prospective. Retrospectively, there is the experience with *Aamodt* and other adjudication suits, which have placed burdens on Hispanic farmers and which many feel have been severely inequitable to their interests. There is widespread sentiment that formal judicial and administrative procedures that treat water exclusively as a commodity do not fit well with the informal, community-oriented practice of water use prevailing among Hispanics.

Prospectively, the increasing value of water in the marketplace and the growing urban and industrial demand in the urban centers lower in the basin increases the probability that an assault will eventually be made on any institutional obstacle to water transfers. Certainly, the *Sporhase* and *El Paso* court cases support that proposition, as does the San Diego County proposal to lease water from the Upper Colorado River Basin. Urban centers appear willing to seek water wherever they can find it, irrespective of previous institutional arrangements. In fact, much of the history of western water, most notably in California, is a record of movement of water in defiance of local sentiment.

An alternative scenario through which a sharply increased demand for water transfers from *acequias* could occur would be a locational decision by a sizable industrial enterprise to build within the Upper Rio Grande region itself because of the availability of water and labor. The latter possibility would more sorely test community concerns for cultural preservation since it would offer the tradeoff of jobs in exchange for a reduction in irrigated agriculture. Out-of-region purchases by a municipality, in contrast, would compensate an individual rightholder but provide little benefit to the community as a whole.

Both prospective scenarios threaten the traditional base of the Hispanic communities in irrigated agriculture, probably more than the threat from adjudication suits that is currently uppermost in the minds of Hispanic farmers and ranchers. Market pressure on traditional water use is virtually certain to grow, whether it be through gradual attrition, as occurs now through occasional sales and transfers even in the face of community opposition, or through some abrupt change caused by a major plant construction initiative or the legal and political collapse of an institutional structure. What is unclear is the speed by which that pressure will build. If "gradual attrition" is the more probable scenario, then the period of increasing pressure will likely extend well into the next century. On the other hand, legal assaults on perceived institutional obstacles to transfers could occur more quickly after careful and secretive preparations by extraregional interests.

More important for the future than the relative probabilities of scenarios about market pressure is the persistence and strength of the community value attached to water in the region. Although it is quite clear that current attitudes about water deplore a strict commodity perspective and emphasize water's importance to the community and traditional Hispanic culture, for most of those communities an actual market test has not occurred. Will community values remain dominant when faced with such a choice? Only future events can give a definitive answer to this question, but we offer some suggestive evidence. Though our survey did not attempt to quantitatively measure the strength of attachment to a particular viewpoint, the vehemence with which community leaders responded to open-ended questions about transfers supports a preservationist sentiment with much depth and strength. The culture provides a sense of identity to many, and the water, as indicated repeatedly in the quotes of Chapter 4, is seen as key to cultural preservation.

The recent Ensenada Ditch[2] case, and particularly the opinion of the district judge, provides further evidence. Developers for a proposed ski resort in the vicinity of Tierra Amarilla in Rio Arriba County purchased water rights appurtenant to land irrigated from an *acequia*, the Ensenada Ditch. The ditch association opposed the transfer not only on the grounds that its water rights would be adversely affected, but also because the proposed transfer was considered inimical to the preservation of the Hispanic culture in the region. Although the State Engineer ruled in favor of the ski development in an administrative hearing, the ditch association appealed to the district court, which heard testimony on the value of the culture and the importance of the water to that culture. The district judge overruled the State Engineer. One excerpt from his opinion is particularly pertinent to this discussion.

> The second main line of argument pits economic values against cultural values. Here, it is simply assumed by the Applicants that greater economic benefits are more desirable than the preservation of a cultural identity. This is clearly not so. Northern New Mexicans possess a fierce pride over their history, traditions and culture. This region of northern New Mexico and its living culture are recognized at the state and federal levels as possessing significant cultural value, not measurable in dollars and cents. The deep-felt and tradition-bound ties of northern New Mexico families to the land and water are central to the maintenance of that culture.

> While these questions seem, at first, far removed from the simple question of the transfer of a few acre feet of water, the evidence discloses a distinct pattern of distruction [sic] of the local culture by development which begins with small, seemingly insignificant steps. I am persuaded that to transfer water rights, devoted for more than a century to agricultural purposes, in order to construct a playground for those who can pay is a poor trade, indeed.[3]

Ironically, the 1985 New Mexico legislature, for reasons unrelated to the ditch case, modified statutes governing transfers to allow public welfare arguments as a basis for contesting transfers.[4] The legislature was concerned with the *El Paso* lawsuit and the rulings of the federal judge in that case, and it is likely that few, if any, legislators foresaw that the first application of a "public welfare" criterion would occur in the Upper Rio Grande on cultural grounds. As of this writing, the district judge's ruling is on appeal, and there is some talk of repealing the public welfare provision. Whatever eventually transpires, however, the decision underscores the strength of cultural preservation concerns.

The Reality of the Agricultural Option

Although Hispanics show a strong preference for agriculture as a water use option, the difficulties involved in an agricultural strategy are substantial. In addition to the problems described in Chapter 7, there are national and regional factors that also loom large. The current health of agriculture in the United States is poor, with farm failures and competitive world markets, among other factors, combining to create a dismal picture. Moreover, as discussed in Chapter 2, the regional prospect is for a shift of water out of irrigated agriculture with a corresponding secular decline in production. Faced with these formidable obstacles, what chance is there for improving the profitability of agriculture in the Upper Rio Grande?

In addressing this question it is important to remember that there have been substantial efforts in the past, as described in Chapter 6, to strengthen the agriculture base of the region. Improving agricultural profitability through conversion to truck crops is not a new idea, and a number of steps in this direction have been tried relatively recently with at best mixed results. For example, an apple cooperative was initiated in the early 1970s but failed at least in part because of a record-setting freeze that destroyed not only most of one year's crop but also a substantial number of the trees themselves. Past efforts show that an agricultural strategy for the Upper Rio Grande is not likely to achieve a dramatic breakthrough whereby the Gordian knot of problems is severed and the future flows smoothly.

A near-term objective of converting three thousand acres or so of farmland to vegetable and fruit crops is, tactically, a more modest and realistic goal. Even this task would not be easy and would require a sustained, coordinated and simultaneous attack on all facets of the problem rather than focusing on one dimension alone. According to agricultural authorities and community leaders familiar with the situation, the following program elements are crucial to success.

1. Community support is essential. For that reason it is almost certainly necessary to channel efforts through the *acequias,* and a community development specialist is probably needed for that purpose.

2. Educational and demonstration efforts are needed. They should probably be directed at the larger growers on the theory

that growers with larger acreage are likely to be more successful in converting to fruits and vegetables with the innovation spreading to smaller farms.

3. Market development is important. The formation of marketing associations is necessary in order to attain sufficient volume to attract buyers and support quality-enhancing steps such as precooling and sorting. Not only should existing growers' markets in Santa Fe and elsewhere be strengthened, but efforts should be made to penetrate established wholesale and retail markets in such places as Albuquerque and Pueblo, Colorado.

4. Water storage capacity and permanent diversion structures are needed. As long as there is inadequate water to irrigate throughout the growing season, then higher-valued, but also higher-risk, crops are unlikely to be grown in sufficient quantity.

These elements do not constitute a detailed plan, nor would they resolve all of the problems that surround Upper Rio Grande agriculture. But, along with the Ganados initiatives, they do capture core prerequisites to improved profitability. The generally unfavorable regional and national environment for agriculture, although certainly a negative factor affecting the possible success of an agricultural strategy, need not be overriding. Success does not require the development of export markets. As long as only nearby markets are sought, local produce in sufficient quality, quantity, and reliability can have some advantages. Moreover, in the long term the gradual decline of regional competitors forecast above is beneficial for those remaining in the business. The truck farming element of the strategy is already succeeding in the northern reaches of the basin, and there are no physical reasons why it should not further south.

In the final analysis, however, the keys to the success of an agricultural strategy are social and organizational. All of the core elements to agricultural redevelopment identified above require social action of some sort. Community support requires assent in some form, and the consequences of not having that assent are very clear from the previous experiences with Llano and Indian Camp. Education and demonstration require some funding as well as some willingness to explore new cropping patterns with the associated burdens of risk and learning time that would be necessary. The marketing component of the strategy for both truck crops and livestock requires capital, but even more importantly requires a willingness to act cooperatively. Investment in water storage and other infrastructure facilities would also take cooperative action, both to develop the source of investment funds and for whatever payback arrangement is necessary.

Whether the necessary degree of social organization is possible is the biggest imponderable associated with an agricultural strategy. The organizational commitment required to implement such a strategy requires an extent of collective enterprise for which the only precedent is the original formation of the *acequias* centuries ago. Although an adequate mechanism conceptually exists in the *acequia* associations, the authority and efficacy required represents a departure from current responsibilities and practice of most *acequias*. There would have to be an extensive revitalization of the *acequias* for this to occur. Moreover, in all likelihood there would need to be an effective organization of *acequias*, at least at the subbasin or community level. The responsibility for making such a commitment remains with the acequias and the individuals and families which they serve.

In order to succeed in their objective of cultural preservation, Hispanics must move from a reactive posture to an active stance of asserting their viewpoint in the water arena and internally organizing to that end. A "business as usual" posture toward the future is likely to produce a further erosion of their traditional water institutions. Yet moving from the path of least resistance is difficult and requires substantial motivation. Both recent history and our survey results reveal a strong motivating attachment to water. Whether it is strong enough to accomplish their objectives is a question for the Hispanic communities themselves to answer.

Hispanics and Pueblos: A Final Note

This case study has focused on the Hispanics in the Upper Rio Grande, yet as the *Aamodt* suit has revealed, the water-related future of the Hispanic communities is closely linked to the water interests of the Pueblos. Though culturally and governmentally distinct, the separate communities have many strong relationships ranging from individual intermarriages to similar holistic perspectives on the value and importance of water. Moreover, while we have not described the situation of the Pueblos in any detail, their economic problems are similar to those of the Hispanics. It is a tragic irony that these two communities have been pitted against one another. Each community of traditional water users has more to gain from a coalition with the other than can occur from contention and conflict.

CHAPTER 9

The Tohono O'odham Nation

The People and Their Land

Today about 14,000 Tohono O'odham live in the Sonoran Desert, their ancestral home and one of the hottest and driest deserts in the Americas. Currently, the O'odham occupy approximately one-third of their aboriginal lands in the United States. Nonetheless, the Tohono O'odham Reservation (see map) is one of the largest Indian reservations in the United States, with a combined area approaching three million acres. O'odham lands are in three units: the main or largest unit, which borders Mexico on the south; the San Xavier Reservation, which shares part of its boundary with that of the city of Tucson; and the tiny Gila Bend Reservation near the non-Indian town of Gila Bend.

Natural resources on the Tohono O'odham Reservation include minerals (principally copper), grazing lands, and irrigable lands. Precipitation is scarce, from five to eight inches on the western side of the main reservation to twelve to eighteen inches in high, eastern mountains, and occurs in two distinct seasons: a summer season of short intense storms and a winter season of longer, more gentle rainfall. Because of high temperatures, the rate of evaporation is extreme. There are no perennial streams. Yet the structural geology of the area is conducive to the storage of groundwater. Small and large groups of mountains are separated by broad basins and valleys, the floors of which are typically lined with porous material.

The Tohono O'odham and Poverty

By most conventional standards, the Tohono O'odham are a poor people. The income distribution among O'odham families

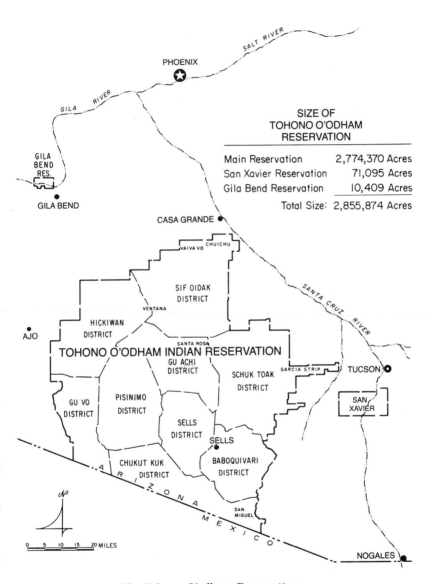

SIZE OF
TOHONO O'ODHAM
RESERVATION

Main Reservation	2,774,370 Acres
San Xavier Reservation	71,095 Acres
Gila Bend Reservation	10,409 Acres
Total Size:	2,855,874 Acres

The Tohono O'odham Reservation

is sharply lower than that in the state of Arizona as a whole. Table 9.1 shows that 46 percent of the resident families on the main reservation earn less than $7,500 a year, whereas fewer than 14 percent of their counterparts statewide are so poor. The mean family income statewide, $22,116, is twice that of the O'odham families, which is only $10,568. The figures for the San Xavier Reservation are slightly higher than the main reservation, but also much lower than for the state as a whole.

Table 9.1. Family Income, 1980

	Tohono O'odham Reservation[a]		State-Wide (all-ethnic groups)[b]	
	No.	%	*No.*	%
<$ 5,000	412	31.0	50,164	7.1
$ 5,000–$ 7,499	200	15.0	45,118	6.4
$ 7,500–$ 9,999	171	12.9	54,552	7.7
$10,000–$14,999	218	16.4	114,870	16.2
$15,000–$19,999	151	11.4	110,812	15.6
$20,000–$24,999	80	6.0	101,285	14.3
$25,000–$34,999	53	4.0	129,897	18.3
$35,000–$49,999	0	0.0	68,964	9.7
>$50,000	0	0.0	34,250	4.8
TOTAL	1,330	100.0	709,912	100.0
MEAN INCOME	$10,568		$22,116	

SOURCES: [a]Adapted from "Socio-Cultural Impact Assessment of the San Xavier Planned Community," Bureau of Applied Research in Anthropology (BARA) (University of Arizona, Tucson, 1984).
[b]Bureau of the Census, *1980 Census of Population,* General Social and Economic Characteristics, Arizona (vol. 1, chap. C, part 4) (Washington, D.C.: U.S. Department of Commerce).

Along with the economic poverty among the Tohono O'odham is a general absence of diverse, independent, and self-sufficient means of livelihood. Welfare, mining lease payments, and government payrolls play a large role in the O'odham economy.[1] Only about 24 percent of working age O'odham men are gainfully employed.[2] Moreover, as Table 9.2 shows, less than 3 percent of those who do work are self-employed. Over 70 percent are employed by some level of government. Two-thirds of these

Table 9.2. Tohono O'odham Employment, Main
Reservation, 1980 (Age 16 and Older)

Class of Employment	No.	%
Private wage and salary	446	24.8
Federal government	579	32.2
State government	166	9.2
Local government	559	31.1
Self-employed	48	2.7
TOTAL	1,798	100.0

SOURCE: Bureau of the Census, *1980 Census of Population*
(Washington, D.C.: U.S. Department of Commerce). Adapted
from BARA, 1984 [see note (a), Table 9.1].

government employees work for the federal and state governments, whose budgets and policies are remote from O'odham
control. Clearly, there is insufficient independent enterprise
and entrepreneurship generating income on the reservation to
alleviate poverty conditions.

The Historical Importance of Water

The saguaro is the ostensive focus of Tohono O'odham ritual,
belief, and activity. Yearly, as the fruits of the giant cactus ripen,
families gather at their desert camps to pick the fruits, prepare
and drink a cactus wine, exchange gossip and food, and observe
the customary rituals associated with the harvest. The success
of the midsummer saguaro harvest has already been insured
by ceremonies and singing during the month of March, the
beginning of spring.[3] The cactus wine, for its part, fosters the
social functions of the harvest camp.

The cactus-wine-drinking ceremony has been largely regarded as responsible for bringing on the rains. Ruth Underhill
wrote: ". . . the liquor had no very high alcoholic content. So
much must be drunk before there is any intoxication that its
most usual effect is to make the drinker vomit. This is recognized as a ceremonial feature, and the people say with pleasure,
pointing out a man so affected: 'Look he is throwing up the
clouds.' The regular procedure during the 24 hours of feast is

to drink, vomit, sleep, and drink again, until the result is a thorough purging."[4] It is an occasion for the O'odham to exert collective power over nature, to control through ritual means a largely unpredictable meteorological event.

The ceremonial efforts of *viikita* had larger purposes. Held every fourth year, the ritual endeavored to "keep the world in order."[5] From the calendar sticks of the Tohono O'odham and the closely related Pimas, there is ample record of the consequences of failing to hold the *viikita*. The oral history associated with the Covered Wells stick records the following, for the year 1882: "It was noted that it was very dry and that "Veeheekita," or the rain feast, had not been properly celebrated, due to the fact that the Indians had been made prosperous by work in the mines. . . . it was decided that if this ceremony should be performed, no more earthquakes would occur and rain would come in abundance. . . . this was done."[6] The ceremony was again allowed to lapse at Covered Wells, so the 1904 entry notes the consequences: "The long neglected "Veeheekita" or rain feast was celebrated this year and the drought was almost immediately broken. There were copious rains and bountiful crops."[7] The timing of events may have been fortuitous. The feelings of efficacy were unquestionably real.

These Sonoran Desert–dwelling people whom the Spaniards encountered in the 1700s were called "Papagos" by the Europeans for ease of reference and administration, but the name had little indigenous validity. Likewise for the neighboring tribe, designated "Pimas." These Uto-Aztecan speakers collectively refer to themselves as "O'odham." The Pimas, living along the Gila River, appropriately called themselves "river people," or *Akimel O'odham*, thus distinguishing their group from the *Tohono O'odham*, the "desert people" of the intermittent washes and mountains to the south. Further south and west, in the desolate mesas of northwest Mexico, a third group of Pima-speakers designated themselves as "sand people" or *Hiaked O'odham*. The Tohono O'odham officially changed their name from "Papago" in 1986. Many quotes and references in this book that pre-date this change use the word "Papago," and some organizations and names (for example, the *Papago Runner*) retain the old designation. Because the Tohono O'odham tribe is the only one of the three that uses the Uto-Aztecan name "O'odham" officially as of this writing, when used alone in this book it refers to that tribe only.

Anthropologists characterize these three groups of Pima-speakers by their dominant modes of subsistence and associated settlement patterns. In the virtual absence of even intermittent flowing water, the "sand people" had to move constantly across the desert, collecting available plants and animals, drinking from the scattered *charcos* (water holes) and rock tanks that filled with rainfall. Under this regime, settled villages were nonexistent, and population was sparse. In contrast to these "no-village" people,[8] the "two-village" people of the Sonoran Desert region maintained semipermanent settlements. These people, the *Tohono O'odham*, were the saguaro gatherers and the *ak chin* ("arroyo mouth") farmers. The winter villages were located in the foothills of desert mountain ranges, near permanent springs. Survival during this season was based on the wild and cultivated surpluses of the summer villages, lower down on the desert floor. Water and resources were more plentiful here than in the west and south, so the "two-village" people could maintain a denser and more sedentary population.

When the saguaro ceremony failed to bring on the required rain, the "two-village" people had to cope quickly. The adaptive pattern that developed out of this necessity was one of mobility. On each side of the central region were "refuge areas," controlled by the riverine-farming "one-villagers." The Gila River and the Santa Cruz River, controlled respectively by the Pima proper and the Pima-speaking Sobaipuri, and the Altar Valley of the Opata in the south were the most attractive areas of refuge for the "two-village" people. Robert Hackenberg describes the functions played by these riverine farming villages:

> Each refuge area was visited by Papagos of a particular regional band who maintained friendly relations with the hosts. The Papago visitors either planted temporary fields near those of their hosts or exchanged labor with them for a share of their crop. In effect this

practice greatly amplified the range of water resources available to the Papago. The headwaters of the three river systems primarily employed (Santa Cruz, Gila, and Altar) were remote from the Papagueria. Given the great variation in the micro-environments of the Southwest, it was highly unlikely that all these locations would suffer from adverse weather conditions at the same time.[9]

Historically, therefore, the Tohono O'odham of the central Sonoran Desert of Arizona—a region called the Papagueria—survived by flexibility and diversification. If the wide range of gathered and cultivated crops failed for lack of rain, the O'odham moved to the refuge areas of flowing rivers. There they exchanged one of their primary resources—their own labor—for crops and goods. Once the season of drought had passed, they then returned to their desert villages and their cactus camps.

Surviving in the Sonoran Desert as the Tohono O'odham successfully did for hundreds of years required highly developed coping strategies. The desert is characterized by variability and change; the O'odham adjusted by accepting high uncertainty as normal and being flexible in their responses. With the onslaught of Anglo culture and technology, however, the Indians found themselves confined to reservations, their traditional patterns of living defunct, faced with a completely new set of survival problems.

In the twentieth century major technological efforts have been made to overcome the uncertainties of rainfall. On Indian reservations, the Indian Service (later the Bureau of Indian Affairs) dug wells, replacing the sporadic rainfall with apparently abundant groundwater. But expanding municipalities adjacent to the reservation jeopardized this source through their own pumping. Now federal agencies and local water users have turned to a new technological solution—the importation of water from the Colorado River.

The origin and response to the Tohono O'odham San Xavier Reservation's water problem, which evolved in the nineteenth century, set a pattern of water policy making that has been followed since. At the beginning of the nineteenth century, the underground flow of Santa Cruz River water surfaced at several points to form springs. One surfacing was at Punta de Agua on the San Xavier Reservation. Area settlers carved *acequias* into the river channel to "intercept the shallow water-table and thus provide a regular water supply in an area where surface supplies were unpredictable and normally inadequate. The ditches headed into the floodplain upstream and were deepest at their headings. Apparently there were no attempts to protect the headings from erosion. If the water-table fell, the gallery would be extended headward and it would be cut deeper into the floodplain."[10]

Effective in seasons of slight river flow, these ditches wreaked havoc on the landscape when the river swelled. By concentrating flood flows and steepening the channel gradient, the artificial ditches enhanced the erosion forces of the river. The Acequia de la Punta de Agua, first noted in 1851, drew water from the surfacing underground flow of the Santa Cruz but quickly initiated erosion. By 1912, the resulting arroyo was sixty to one hundred feet wide, six to twenty feet deep, and two miles long. Similar effects were noted along the main branch of the river. The nearby Eastside Barranca, for example, reached a length of two miles, and the Tucson Arroyo downstream, initiated in 1887 by pioneer Sam Hughes's irrigation ditch, was eighteen miles long in 1912. In the process of upstream entrenchment, Hughes's legacy cut into the San Xavier Reservation, destroying some 150 acres of Tohono O'odham fields.[11]

In addition to scarring the surface, the developing arroyos affected the underground water supply. The water table dropped to the level of the deepened channel, thus stopping the flow to the previously running springs. The entrenching channels also accelerated river runoff; less water infiltrated the underlying aquifer. By 1912, neither the ephemeral surface flow nor the subterranean stream of the Santa Cruz provided sufficient water to irrigate fields of the growing town of Tucson.

The responses of the Indians and non-Indians to their common problem of interrupted water supply followed different patterns that became characteristic. The non-Indian farmers and town dwellers sunk wells into the aquifer. The O'odham, without funds of their own, sought out their Indian agents to dig the wells for them. The Indian Service complied, but the wells were too few, and too poorly maintained, to revive farming on the San Xavier Reservation.

The disappointment of the Tohono O'odham with federal responses to their need for wells was symptomatic of more general difficulties with federal Indian policies. Indeed, problems went beyond simple lack of responsiveness to include federal constraint upon what the O'odham could do for themselves to develop economically.

Past federal Indian policy has placed a number of constraints on Indian participation in decision making both on and off the reservation. Historic policies, such as the reservation policy and the control over the reservations assumed by the Indian Bureau, denied the Indians control over their own economic resources. The dependency relationship that resulted from the Indians being forced to rely on the government for subsistence hindered Indian political and economic development. Other federal policies, such as the Indian Reorganization Act, imposed a tribal bureaucracy on many tribes that hindered the participation of the individual Indian in decision making on the reservation itself.

CHAPTER 10

Tohono O'odham Participation in Water Resource Development: Constraints and Opportunities

Introduction

The key ingredient in the success of economic development projects the world over is the participation of the poor themselves in solving their own problems.[1] The previous chapter demonstrated that historically the Tohono O'odham actively participated in a complex and flexible strategy for coping with the vagaries of water supply in the desert. Along with their participation came feelings of efficacy and control. The arrival of Anglos and the confinement of the O'odham to a reservation system was accompanied by a loss of control over natural resources. Until recently, the Bureau of Indian Affairs (BIA) and non-Indians, through leasing of reservation lands, dominated resource decisions. Because these decisions were governmental and political, the effective avenues for participation of the O'odham necessarily became political. Yet, the O'odham were hampered in their political participation by a federal agency unable or unwilling to protect Indian interests and lacking in the bureaucratic skills and resources to act effectively. Further, the participation of Indians was limited because they were denied choice of governing structure and the process for expressing their views and preferences.

The legacy of federal Indian policy is the erosion of the historic participation through which the Tohono O'odham acted to insure their own well-being. Nowhere is the inheritance of federal constraints upon participation more obvious than in the O'odham's lack of success in securing and developing water resources.

The Federal Responsibility

The responsibility for the development and protection of the water on the reservation falls on the BIA. The federal trust responsibility to the Indians requires that the federal government, as the trustee, "exercise the care, diligence, and skill of a prudent person in managing the trust assets of the beneficiary."[2] This duty of the government extends to the protection of water resources. But, consistently over the last one hundred years, the BIA has failed to protect the Tohono O'odham water supply; in fact, tribal dependence upon the bureau has burdened O'odham action.

Throughout its existence, the BIA has always been short of funds and also has spent a large percentage of its budget on administration, rather than on the reservation itself. As a result, the bureau has stressed leasing over the development of Indian lands and has been reluctant to expend the needed capital for wells and a distribution system. Further complicating matters for the O'odham, very few private lending institutions will lend water development money to Indians because their land is held in trust and cannot be used as collateral for a loan.

The Historical Record

The Early 1900s

In 1917, a key decision was made by the bureau that held many consequences for Tohono O'odham farming and the protection of the tribal water supply. In that year, the bureau "quit the pumps."[3] As the government farmer for San Xavier reported, "I understood it was too expensive for the government to keep those pumps in operation. They quit operating them and undertook to develop a gravity supply of water."[4] In 1929, this gravity system was destroyed when a section of pipe caved in, leaving the San Xavier O'odham without water to irrigate.[5] The government, aside from investigations, took no steps to replace the system.[6] Instead, the bureau told the Indians that only if they began to grow cotton, a crop the government believed "will bring them substantial returns," instead of beans and other food supplies, would the bureau be inclined to replace it.[7] As a result, in 1931 the O'odham had only one-fifth of the previous water supply provided by the pumps and could irrigate only one hundred to three hundred acres of the two thousand that otherwise could be cultivated. A severe shortage of water continued on the reservation, and the O'odham, dependent on the government to dig new wells, reported as major problems "their stock dying for lack of water"[8] and "a lack of irrigation water."[9]

Recent Decades

Although the Civilian Conservation Corps (CCC) constructed improvements, such as new wells, on the Tohono O'odham Reservation in the 1930s, World War II brought a halt to most development plans as funds were channeled away from the reservation to support the war effort. Afterward, progress was very slow even in livestock development, the BIA's major program. By 1955, "only 14,000 cattle [the same number as in 1934] were being supported on the Papago Indian Reservation, and only 40% of the range was within reach of permanent water."[10] Many tribal members began to work off-reservation, either picking cotton or working in the mines.

The 1950s marked the beginning of a rapid decline in groundwater levels. The use of water became increasingly dependent on capital as groundwater levels dropped and much larger sums of money were needed to build deeper wells and to operate and maintain them. The bureau's continued failure to develop an adequate water supply for the reservation meant that non-Indians were able to pump from the common pool of groundwater that served both Anglos and Indians.

Droughts throughout the 1960s decimated the cattle industry as *charcos* dried up, leaving the cattle to die of thirst. With tribal members primarily dependent on ranching for their income, the reservation was thrust further into poverty as most Indians did not make an *annual* family income of twenty-four hundred dollars in 1970.[11]

Although other non-Indian cattlemen also suffered from the drought and were forced to cut back, the Tohono O'odham and their cattle starved primarily because they, unlike non-Indians, were still dependent on the desert for water. In 1969, over twelve hundred cattle lay dead on the reservation, with thousands more sold at a loss. The livestock died by the hundreds from a shortage of food and water throughout 1970. The lack of rainfall was responsible for the *charcos* drying up, but unlike non-Indian cattlemen, the O'odham had few wells to use as a backup, and those that were working were threatened by the rapidly dropping water table. The reservation director of maintenance reported in 1969 that "sometimes we won't hear about a well being out for months. We have 11 wells in disrepair. Most of them have water in them but we can't get parts to repair them, and sometimes we don't have the equipment to fix them even if we did have the parts."[12] A tribal request in 1969 to the bureau for $424,710 to cover long-range development of livestock and alleviate the drought was refused. Instead, the Interior Department set aside $50,000 for this effort and only granted $37,500.[13]

The Tat Momolikot Dam

The Tohono O'odham's usual treatment from the federal government was too little water development too late. When the infrequent federal effort at water development on the reservation did occur, it was of dubious value.

In the summer of 1975, the Army Corps of Engineers completed a project that promised to provide an adequate water supply and a recreational facility for the O'odham on the western part of the reservation. This project, the Tat Momolikot Dam, was conceived in 1962 by the corps after a devastating flood wiped out the non-Indian cotton fields west of Casa Grande, causing an estimated $3.4 million in damages.[14] The corps, with the help of the BIA, the National Park Service, and the Department of Housing and Urban Development, as well as the backing of Casa Grande farmers, "set to work selling the Tat Momolikot Dam project to the Tohono Tribe soon after the 1962 flood," with Thomas St. Clair, superintendent of the reservation, "pushing for all he was worth."[15] The benefits promised included (1) a thirty-six-hundred-acre lake behind the dam; (2) facilities to accommodate fishermen, sailors, and other recreationists; and (3) other tourist facilities, including ramadas and parking areas.[16]

Today, the land behind the Tat Momolikot Dam is typically covered with only inches of water. It would take a "monster flood," "statistically more than 100 years away," to form a lake behind the dam.[17] Even smaller rains of the 25-year or 50-year type would do no more than deposit a few inches of water behind the dam, leaving the body of water "unsuitable for any recreation other than barefoot walking."[18] The dam provides no benefits for the Indians for whom it was built. One tribal member asserts that it was built only "for the benefit of the Anglo farmers, of the Casa Grande area, who wanted protection from a repeat of the 1962 flood" and because it "would help recharge their falling underground water table."[19]

The Tat Momolikot Dam was the largest water project ever attempted on the reservation, and it still left the O'odham thirsty at a loss of $11.7 million. This project was conceived and built with almost no tribal participation. The "lake" behind the project was named "Lake St. Clair," after the superintendent of the reservation. The dedication ceremony was planned to coincide with the Army Corps of Engineers' two hundredth anniversary and to feature Congressman Morris Udall as the keynote speaker. The tribe, including the whole tribal leadership, was not invited. Only after the O'odham complained was it cancelled. From the beginning to the end, the O'odham were excluded from the planning of this project.

Tucson's Threat to Tohono O'odham Water

The disappointment the Tohono O'odham may have felt about the federal government's failure to develop water resources in ways responsive to their needs should have been—and eventually was—accompanied by alarm over a second, associated failure. The federal government failed to protect the store of groundwater beneath O'odham lands from exploitation by others.

The groundwater found in the Upper Santa Cruz Basin, the aquifer that runs beneath the San Xavier Reservation, became a valuable resource for the city of Tucson early in its history. Although O'odham land was protected from further settlement when it was designated a reservation, it was still seen as a potential source of water by non-Indian settlers. By 1881, the Tucson Water Company had drilled a number of wells just west of San Xavier in order to provide the city with a supply of water.[20] From this point forward the city would continue to develop this well field to fuel Tucson's high growth rate. By 1964, the city was withdrawing 165,000 acre-feet of water a year, causing an overdraft of more than 90,000 acre-feet a year.[21] By the 1970s, approximately 40,000 acre-feet of water were supplied annually by the pumps located just outside of the reservation.

In 1930, the city of Tucson purchased a tract of land located just north of the San Xavier Reservation specifically "for purposes of water development."[22] The chief irrigation engineer of San Xavier, Herbert V. Clotts, warned the commissioner of Indian affairs that any development by the city in this area would endanger the water supply permanently and that "this is a matter which should be handled by the Department of Justice with all possible dispatch and vigor."[23] The Catholic mission suggested that the government acquire this land for the Indians in order to protect the water supply of San Xavier.[24]

But the bureau, reluctant to spend monies on the reservation, began to negotiate with the city. In 1931, Mayor G. K. Smith of Tucson, stating that the city needed a source of water and that the Santa Cruz Valley has the "largest and most valuable source of water for Tucson,"[25] suggested a project to benefit Indians and non-Indians. Smith proposed that the city be allowed to pump water off of San Xavier in excess of "10,000,000 gallons per day for 50,000 people at 200 gallons per capita."[26] In return, the city would develop an irrigation system for 2,000 acres on San Xavier. Father Oblasser of Sells spoke against this plan, arguing that "to pay 10,000,000 gallons daily for pumping and delivery of 4 acre-feet for 2,000 acres does seem an exorbitant price."[27]

Although this project was never completed, it is illustrative of the bureau's failure to protect the Tohono O'odham's water supply. By discontinuing the pumps on San Xavier in 1917, the bureau left the Indians without an adequate water supply and made them more susceptible to unfavorable projects such as the one proposed by the city. Although warned by the chief irrigation engineer at San Xavier that any development on the land the city purchased would permanently endanger the O'odham water supply, the bureau took no action to protect it, either through litigation or land purchase. Instead, the city continued to pump water from under lands surrounding the reservation.

Lack of Decision-Making Mechanisms

When the Indian Reorganization Act (IRA) was passed in 1934, the Tohono O'odham had little familiarity with the Anglo systems of representative government. The League of Papago Chiefs, a tribal organization composed of chiefs from many parts of the reservation, managed most internal conflicts, administered some government programs, and often acted in a semiofficial capacity with the neighboring Anglo settlers. The political organization of the O'odham stemmed from village and community rather than the tribe, with the latter unit having little indigenous validity, as discussed in Chapter Nine.

The constitution drawn up under the IRA established eleven political districts, largely based on the nine existing grazing districts of the Sells (Main) Reservation plus San Xavier and Gila Bend.[28] Each of the districts elected its own council, of which two delegates would represent the district on the tribal council. The members of this council then would elect the chair, vice-chair, secretary, and treasurer.

Although some Tohono O'odham traditions were incorporated into the constitution, the document was basically modeled after the Constitution of the United States. Most of the power over lands was given to the council. The council had control over all tribal lands, including the communally held village lands, the power to change district boundaries, and the power to regulate family relations, matters of inheritance, and the disposition of property.[29] More importantly, the tribal council under the IRA was given exclusive control over funds received from the federal government. This provision had long-term effects on the reservation, particularly by creating a *tribal* bureaucracy. Before the IRA, the focus of political organization was the village, with elders responsible for governance.[30] In this indigenous form of government—a "Papago democracy"[31]—decisions were reached through consensus building, not majority rule or elections, and decisions were reached slowly, only after all affected parties had discussed an issue. This process served to diffuse opposition and build support for the final outcome.

For many years after passage of the IRA, the O'odham were able to incorporate this consensus-building dimension of their cultural form of decision making into the new form of government mandated by the act. But as the older chiefs died and the village councils disappeared, no mechanism existed on the reservation that enabled a consensus to form. Traditional patterns of decision making were difficult to sustain as financial pressures and the non-Indian world continued to impact the reservation.

Members of the tribal council, however, soon came to be regarded as "messengers between the different levels of government rather than as spokesmen clothed with authority to act on behalf of the village."[32] In this role, the council had to implement unpopular programs of the bureau, such as stock and horse reduction. They had to make decisions in a non-Indian framework, on a non-Indian timetable. It is precisely this clash between the indigenous culture and Anglo ways that most affected the tribal council. It was very difficult for the tribal council to promote participation among the villages while working essentially on a non-Indian schedule.

Constituency expectations for tribal council members and reelection exigencies also served to undercut indigenous participation. Because a tribe's survival often depended on the steady influx of federal funds, tribal leaders were forced to form a "Washington connection."[33] Tribal leaders, perceiving that they "must keep getting something for their constituents since they want to remain in office,"[34] were forced to sustain and nurture relations with federal agencies in order to ensure continued funds for tribal programs. Key supporters of tribal council members were rewarded with jobs. In 1980 almost a third of the employed O'odham worked for the tribe (see Table 9.2 in Chapter 9), and as one tribal member noted, "Right now with the tribe it's really political."[35] In sum, the connection between the villages and the tribal council member's reelection was continued funding and jobs as rewards for supporters. Patronage, not necessarily shared opinions, linked those elected by the voters.

Non-Indian economic and political pressures also placed constraints on the ability of the Tohono O'odham to reach decisions through consensus. In the late 1960s, shortly after Office of Economic Opportunity (OEO) funds became available, O'odham decision making was changed. In response to concerns of the tribal attorney, a committee system was introduced.[36] This change was not without cost. As one former council member explained: "So now they propose some[thing] and they send it to committee, and supposedly each committee is representing the people, saying 'okay.' So they leave out the people. They [outsiders dealing with the tribe] just work with the council and the committees, and most of the time the committee is the council themselves. They're particular who they have in those committees."[37] As one observer noted, this change in O'odham government essentially "short-circuited direct and meaningful village involvement in tribal affairs."[38]

Among the primary motivations underlying the adoption of a new constitution by the Tohono O'odham Nation in 1986 was a desire to facilitate participation. The dominance of the council was checked by a strengthened executive and judiciary. Provisions were included for impeachment and recall of corrupt officials or those with whom voters are dissatisfied. The people themselves can now propose or defeat legislation through initiative and referendum.[39] Whether the new constitution will have the effect of bringing the government of the Tohono O'odham Nation closer to the grass roots remains to be seen. It is particularly difficult to foresee whether the new constitution will have much effect on the patronage relations between the council and constituencies.

Prior to the constitutional change in 1986, however, a gap

clearly existed between the tribal council and the villages. Empowered by the IRA and required to interact with the non-Indian work, the tribal council had lost some of its ties with the villages. In contrast, the villages, although no longer retaining their councils,[40] still relied on the consensus-building mode of decision making. Whereas the tribal council was often forced to respond to the issues on a non-Indian timetable, with a "yes" or "no" answer, the local people continued to settle issues in the districts through discussion and consensus, and they often took a long time to do it. This division was evidenced by the tortuous process through which a land development lease (discussed below) was considered. The tribal council, district council, and allottees took different stances at different times, undoubtedly providing fuel for the constitutional modification that occurred in 1986.

O'odham Legal Claims to Water:
The Opportunity for Leverage

As demonstrated, the Tohono O'odham have had little control over the development of their water resources and have been plagued by severe shortages of water on the reservation. This situation is ironic, for on paper, the Indian tribes are the largest water rightholders in the West. A formidable body of law exists that gives the Indians of Arizona, including the O'odham, the right to claim ownership to much of the water in Arizona.

The Indian tribes' legal rights to water have been recognized for over three-quarters of a century. In the 1908 *Winters* decision,[41] the Supreme Court held that Indians "have prior and paramount rights to all water resources which arise upon, border, traverse, or underlie a reservation" in sufficient quantity to satisfy present and future needs of a reservation.[42] These *Winters* rights predate the rights held by most other water users who acquired their water under state law, and are open-ended since the future needs of the tribes must be considered.

For over fifty years after *Winters* was decided, the *Winters* doctrine was almost ignored by the states. The Colorado River Compact of 1922, as mentioned in Chapter 1, allocated no

water to the Indian tribes. In addition, most of the federal reclamation projects built in Arizona also ignored Indian claims.
Few states directly challenged the legality of *Winters* claims,
choosing instead to develop water and put it to use under the
doctrine of prior appropriation. But in 1963, another Supreme
Court decision, *Arizona v. California*,[43] forced the states to
include Indian water rights in future planning.

In this historic case, the Court, in deciding how the waters
of the lower Colorado River should be allocated, quantified Indian water rights for the Colorado River tribes using "practically
irrigable acreage" as the standard. Because Indian rights had
never been quantified before, their extent had been unknown.
Under this new standard, however, the Colorado River tribes
alone were awarded 905,496 acre-feet of reserved water, a considerable share of the annual flow of the Colorado. Under this
same standard the Indian tribes of Arizona, with a land base
of approximately 19.4 million acres, could claim "more than
ten times the amount of the annual dependable supply of water
in the state even if only one-third of the reservation lands were
'practically irrigable.'"[44]

Another case in 1976, *Cappaert v. United States*,[45] further
strengthened the Indian tribes' legal claim to water. The Supreme Court for the first time in this case extended the concept
of reserved water rights to protect against groundwater withdrawals affecting surface water uses. Potentially, *Winters* reserved rights might be extended to apply to groundwater. Unquestionably this ruling bolstered the position of the O'odham.

At the same time the court decisions were favoring Indians,
great strides were being made in sharpening legal skills. Indian
lawyers became more adept at pressing their water claims, and
numerous lawsuits began to be filed in the federal courts. One
writer described the question of tribal water entitlements as
"the sword of Damocles that hangs over the West."[46]

Developments through the courts provided the Tohono
O'odham resources they could use to gain entry to the local
water policy arena. Shut out from the use of the water because
of a lack of funds and years of inadequate BIA trusteeship, the
tribe had previously had little influence in decisions concerning

water use in the Tucson Basin. Other, more politically powerful interests such as the city, the mines, and agricultural interests developed water resources as they were needed to support continued economic growth. But on the basis of the *Winters* doctrine, *Arizona v. California,* and the *Cappaert* case, the O'odham could legally claim most of the available water in the Tucson Basin. Non-Indian interests were threatened with a halt of economic growth, jeopardized bond ratings, difficulties in getting private loans, and potential reallocation of water to the Tohono O'odham. Encouraged by their strong legal position, the O'odham confronted non-Indian economic interests and, as we see in Chapter 11, used a previously unenforceable court doctrine to draw all interests to the negotiating table.

CHAPTER 11

The Tohono O'odham
Take Initiative

The Tohono O'odham File Suit

In 1975, when San Xavier's water table had been "sucked so low that new wells hit dry bedrock,"[1] the federal government, on behalf of the O'odham, filed suit against the city of Tucson, mining companies, and agricultural interests. Claiming reserved rights and aboriginal rights, the tribe contended that the federal government had failed to perform its obligations under the *Winters* doctrine and that the tribe's water rights had been damaged by the excessive pumping of the defendants.

At this point, the O'odham had at least two choices: seek a negotiated settlement or press the suit to its resolution. Because of a strong legal position, Indian tribes have traditionally sought the adjudication of their water rights in the federal courts. The *Winters* doctrine and other court decisions gave the O'odham a strong chance of winning their case, thereby favoring the litigation alternative.

Other factors pressed the tribe toward negotiation. First, the suit could prove to be extremely expensive. Because of the appeals expected, the case promised to drag on for ten to twenty years. Second, there was no guarantee that any available water would be left in the basin in twenty years. As one local attorney commented, no court is "going to enjoin Pima County out of existence. . . . the Papago may be looking at getting money instead of water."[2] Finally, even if the tribe were granted rights to groundwater, they still needed money to develop the water. Cuts in federal funding and the reluctance of private bankers to loan money to Indian tribes meant that the O'odham may not be able to develop any water received through the courts.

There was strong support among the collective defendants for a negotiated settlement of the O'odham's claims to be financed by legislative appropriation. Despite considerable anger over the suit, the strength of the claim was widely recognized and the cost of an adverse judgment simply too high. In perhaps exaggerated terms, the *Arizona Daily Star* editorialized: "More than a century of government failure to preserve the Papagos' interests assured the tribe of a court victory. And victory for the Papagos could have meant the permanent shutdown of mines and farms and an end to city growth and development."[3] The suit acted as "a cloud, a club over everybody."[4] Tucson's bond rating was even in jeopardy because of the unknown quantity of Indian claims.

In 1980, the original suit was amended to include another 1,750 local water users as defendants.[5] Every major water user in the basin, from the Catholic Church to the Boy Scouts of America, was named in the suit.[6] Called a "blunderbuss, an incredible engine to use to solve a social problem—Indian rights versus whites," the suit promised to be a "can of worms and a Pandora's box" for area water users.[7] At the minimum, the suit would have cost local water users $437,500 just for the initial paperwork involved in answering the complaint.[8]

With the filing of the lawsuit, the O'odham gained entry into the local water policy arena. As William Strickland, the tribe's attorney, noted:

> It's very difficult to get a meeting. I'll guarantee you that the agriculturalists of this state, including FICO [a large corporate farming enterprise], we'd have to use a piece of dynamite or something to get them to sit down and talk, really seriously talk, in open communications about these problems. When you get rebuffed a hundred and fifty times, you're not going to go back and knock on the door, and if somebody criticizes you, you're not going to be knocking the hundred and fifty-first time.[9]

The "piece of dynamite" proved to be the "grim reality of the Winters doctrine."[10] Because the suit threatened the economic interests of the politically powerful groups in the Tucson Basin, the O'odham were able to take this previously unenforceable court doctrine and use it to secure a place at the bargaining table. For the first time, the tribe was in a position to participate in decisions affecting its water rights, and the tribe turned its attention toward negotiation.

Negotiations Begin

In the legal arena, the O'odham had a number of resources, primarily the *Winters* doctrine and a well-prepared lawsuit. In Congress, however, they lacked the money, votes, lobbying skills, and united front necessary to succeed. The O'odham needed the support and political resources of local interests. But their suit had generated a lot of conflict in the Tucson area. To obtain the power and influence in Congress that the non-Indian interests could provide, the tribe needed to resolve these conflicts with local water users.

In January 1978, William Strickland invited the major water users in eastern Pima County to meet informally on a weekly basis in order to negotiate a legislative settlement of the tribe's water rights.[11] This initiative eventually evolved into the Water Resources Coordinating Committee (WRCC), with substantial funding from various sources. During the first year of negotiations, key administrative and policy decisions were made. It was not until December, however, that the membership of the group was determined. Members included a representative and an alternate from the groups listed in Table 11.1.[12]

The group evolved the stated goal "to develop a fair and reasonable water resources plan which will satisfy the present and future water needs of eastern Pima County."[13] Other aims included a reduction in the groundwater overdraft, an increase in the water resources available to Pima County, and of course, support for "a speedy resolution of Papago Indian water rights claims."[14]

This broader purpose for the WRCC is of major importance, for it is indicative of the preoccupation of Tucson area water interests with extending the Central Arizona Project (CAP) to Tucson and of their awareness that an O'odham settlement

Table 11.1. Membership on the Water Resources
              Coordinating Committee

Agriculture (3)	Avra Valley Land Owners Assoc.; Cortaro-Marana Irrigation District; Farmers Investment Co., Inc. (FICO)
Mines (4)	Anamax Mining Co.; ASARCO, Inc.; Cyprus-Pima Mining Co.; Duval Corp.
Municipal (2)	City of Tucson; Pima County
Indian (3)	Tohono O'odham Indian Tribe; Tohono O'odham allottees;[a] Bureau of Indian Affairs
Other (4)	Tucson Electric Power Co.; University of Arizona; Davis-Monthan Air Force Base; U. S. Army Corps of Engineers
Private citizen	Betsy Zukowski and alternate Jon Sebba

[a]Individual Tohono O'odham landowners on the reservation originally created by the Dawes Act of 1880.

could be instrumental to this end. Not only could the adverse consequences of an unfavorable court decision be avoided, but the federal trust responsibility to the O'odham could be used as an additional lever for federal funding.

There was simply no way the tribe's water claims could be met through existing water supplies in Pima County, without a reallocation of water. President Carter's "hit list" of water projects included the CAP, and there was speculation in Tucson that the aqueduct to Tucson might never be completed. The members of the WRCC, by eventually tying the settlement of the Indian claims to the construction of the CAP, could seize a good opportunity to guarantee that the CAP would be built and thus fulfill O'odham claims without a reallocation of water.

Secretary Andrus and the CAP

Outside pressure from the Interior Department in 1979 and 1980 also influenced negotiations at the local level. In 1979, Cecil B. Andrus, secretary of interior under President Carter, warned that forthcoming CAP allocations would be contingent on "the adequacy of the groundwater reforms adopted by the State of Arizona"[15] and "secure negotiated settlements to outstanding Indian water rights claims in Central Arizona."[16]

Although he denied that the CAP was being held hostage to the Indian interest, he also cautioned that (1) "the Secretary has the legal authority to change the allocation" and (2) "a reallocation may occur if Indian water rights cannot be resolved any other way."[17] Andrus was applying pressure to settle Indian claims because he wanted to make final CAP allocations before he left office.

The climate in Washington, in the Congress and the new administration, was becoming increasingly hostile to big water projects like the CAP. Senator Daniel Patrick Moynihan (New York) and Senator Howard Metzenbaum (Ohio) proposed that money for reclamation projects be cut by $200 million to $300 million a year.[18] David Stockman, incoming head of the Office of Management and Budget (OMB), proposed numerous budget cuts in all areas of government, including water projects.[19] Tucson feared that unless action was taken the Tucson Aqueduct might never be built. As Morris Udall, Tucson congressman and chairman of the House Interior Committee, noted at the time, the CAP aqueduct to Tucson was just a line on a piece of paper. "There has got to be a bill this year that says the aqueduct is so big . . . and here is a plan to settle and quantify the Indian water claims."[20] Taken together, a number of forces worked toward successful local negotiations. Tucson needed the CAP built, and Andrus refused to make final allocations unless the Indian claims were settled. Also, it was to Tucson's advantage for the Indians to receive CAP water. If the water claims of the O'odham were settled through a legislative settlement, Congress would be obligated to deliver the water or pay damages. Not only would the city get a guarantee that the CAP would be built, the water would be cheaper and more accessible for local water users.

In 1981, local water users and the O'odham presented testimony to members of Congress at two congressional hearings held in Tucson. The resulting "consensus bill" was introduced as H.R. 5118 in the House on December 3, 1981, signaling a shift of negotiations to the national arena. On March 4, 1982, H.R. 5118 passed the House of Representatives by a vote of 311–50, due to the influence of Udall in the House and the united front in Pima County supporting the settlement.[21] The lopsided vote in the House gave little forewarning of opposition from two sources that arose during Senate hearings. First, Garrey Carruthers, assistant secretary of interior for land and water resources, queried, "Why should Americans in Boston and South Dakota pay to resolve a problem that belongs principally to Arizona?"[22] He objected to the bill on the grounds that the bill required too much of a contribution from the federal government. The other opposition came from members of the Tohono O'odham Nation.

Tohono O'odham Participation and Representation

The roots of O'odham opposition emerging so late in the legislative process can be traced to issues concerning O'odham representation and participation first raised in Chapter 10. Questions arise as to the extent to which the O'odham actually participated in local bargaining. The membership list and attendance records of the WRCC provide one measure. The O'odham had three representatives on the WRCC. They were represented by their attorney, William Strickland, who attended well over 80 percent of the meetings and spoke on behalf of the tribe. Undoubtedly, given the complexity of the negotiations, Strickland played a major role throughout the process.

O'odham allottees and the Bureau of Indian Affairs each had a representative on the committee. First Mark Ulmer and subsequently Tom Berning stood in for allottees and attended approximately 50 percent of the meetings. The BIA representative rarely attended the meetings, attributing his absence to lack of travel funds. Since the BIA could have linked local negotiations to Washington bureaucracy in the Department of Interior, the absence was notable.

The tribal chairman attended a few meetings of the WRCC and later presented testimony at congressional hearings. In addition, the six-member Papago [now Tohono O'odham] Water Commission was formed and identified as the group "to coordinate with in establishing suitable plans for further negotiations." In light of the O'odham opposition that arose at the Senate hearing, it is necessary to raise the question of whether the tribal council, water commission, and tribal representatives on the WRCC were adequate Indian representatives. An answer is difficult. The O'odham are hesitant to criticize tribal leaders in public. The *Papago Runner*, the tribal newspaper, did report that "some saw the action as literally giving up federally guaranteed rights to groundwater."[23] Other tribal members questioned the projected availability of CAP water.[24] How widespread this sentiment was is unknown. Whether the WRCC was sufficiently sensitive to tribal opinion is also uncertain. Other, more politically powerful groups were certainly more able to shape the issues on the agenda than were the O'odham. The O'odham had at least "partial" participation, or the ability to *influence* the decision-making process, though they lacked the power to shape the issues being considered.[25] At any point, they could have reactivated the suit if the negotiated agreement had been unacceptable.

Near the end of 1980, before H.R. 5118 had been formulated, some members of the WRCC had questioned the group's representativeness and future. A questionnaire was circulated, and among the results the importance of O'odham participation was recognized. "Without Papago participation, there is a void in what the committee can do."[26]

Clearly, the tribal members who testified against legislation in the Senate did not feel the bill reflected their interests. Two representatives of the Gu Vo District traveled to Washington for the express purpose of opposing the settlement. Two weeks before the Senate hearing, the Gu Vo District Council had passed a resolution against the bill and stated that it would not accept "money, services, or entitlements for the bill."[27] At the hearing, the two men presented the opposing resolution, which made four points.

1. The waiver of water rights would "weaken our position of future, potential water claims and affect future descendants of the Western District."
2. The district also opposed setting a precedent for the "whole Indian nation" and stated that "although the tribal council has never been shown letters of opposition, it has been clear that such letters were sent to the tribal administration and that several tribes are opposed to the act."

3. The district also stated that under their interpretation of the
   Leavitt Act, the entire tribe, not just San Xavier and Schuk Toak,
   would be responsible for the debt incurred from the cost of the
   delivery of the water.
4. "Throughout the whole process and the progress to the act, from
   its initial draft to its present status, the tribal council has been
   presented with the positive aspects during the July meeting. Mr.
   Mark Ulmer offered his opinion and analysis of the act, the tribal
   council passed resolution 86-81, requesting that such analysis
   be prepared and submitted for council consideration. This
   analysis has yet to be presented to the tribal council, or any of
   the districts directly involved in the act."[28]

The analysis referred to in point 4, entitled *Discussion Paper:
Southern Arizona Water Rights Settlement Act of 1981*, was
prepared by Mark Ulmer at the request of the tribal council. In
an interview, Ulmer explained his involvement:

> Periodically, I would appear before the tribal council and prepare
> data to penetrate Strickland's data, especially concerning the quality
> and availability of Colorado River Water. The council started to split
> over the question, and my solution was to prepare a document which
> would clarify the problems. This was passed unanimously, and I
> spent seven months researching and preparing the document. By
> the time I finished it, the bill had been introduced, but I maintain
> that there was still time to consider and use it. The paper was given
> to the Chairman, Strickland, and the commission. I don't think any
> of them read it. There was not enough money in Papago legal services
> to give copies to the tribal council members. Three months went by
> and I realized that the information was not passed to the tribal
> council. It was not passed to the people of San Xavier, and not to
> the Water Commission.[29]

Evidently, although consensus may have been reached among
local water users, controversy continued on the reservation.

Despite the Gu Vo opposition, the bill passed the Senate on
a voice vote and, after House concurrence in Senate amend-
ments, went to the president. Ronald Reagan signed a veto
message on June 1, 1982. Calling H.R. 5118 "a negotiated
settlement with a serious flaw," Reagan objected to the bill on
the grounds that the "United States government was never a
party to the negotiations."[30] Fearing that the federal government would bear the total cost of the settlement, which he
pegged at $112 million with an annual cost of $5 million,

Reagan called the bill "a multi-million dollar bail-out of local public and commercial interests at the expense of federal tax-payers throughout the nation."[31] He would, however, consider new legislation reflecting the participation of the federal government.

Recognizing the impossibility of congressional override, an angry Congressman Morris Udall sent an eight-page letter to President Reagan, requesting a federal negotiator. Criticizing Reagan's position that the federal government was not involved in the negotiations, Udall observed that "communities like Tucson are in a 'Catch-22' posture: the President will not sign a settlement that has not had active participation from the U.S. government; but there is no policy, no office of negotiations, no coordinated program for such participation."[32] In response, Reagan appointed Bill Horn, a deputy undersecretary in the Interior Department, to head a negotiating team. This panel also included William H. Coldiron, interior solicitor; Robert Broadbent, Bureau of Reclamation head; Ken Smith, commissioner of the BIA; and other officials from the Interior Department.[33]

New Negotiations in Tucson

How the costs of the settlement were to be shared was the central issue, and after disposing of most elements, the negotiations reached an impasse over a critical feature of the act, the cost of *not* delivering the water to the Tohono O'odham.[34] This issue was of critical importance to the tribe. Water experts agreed that there would be shortage years on the Colorado River, during which the O'odham would not receive their full CAP water entitlement. The federal government would then be obligated to pay damages to the tribe for the nondelivery of water. It was extremely difficult to estimate these damages because they were based on a number of factors, including "the amount of water that would be available in water short years, how often the shortages would occur, and how many Papago Indians will be losing money if they don't have water."[35] But state and federal officials disagreed over just how frequently shortages would occur. If tribal farms were forced to shut down for a lack of water, the tribe wanted to be compensated not only for the value of the water lost but also for other consequential damages: lost income, lost jobs, and other derived farm income. As Strickland noted: "It's a question of jobs. People want to work. That's why we wanted water instead of money in the first place."[36] As a result of these uncertainties, estimates ranged from $1.6 million to $3.7 million a year for shortage years.[37] After considerable negotiation and further congressional action, a final compromise was reached through clarifying language in the conference report: "In the event available income on the [trust] fund [established] is insufficient in any given year to pay damages under Section 304(c) and 305(d), Congress in that year may appropriate additional monies for the fund for such purposes, or the tribe may seek a determination of damages in excess of payments made in the Court of Claims under Section 1505 of Title 28, U.S.C."[38]

On October 12, 1982, after both the House and Senate agreed to the conference legislation, President Reagan signed into law the revised version of the Southern Arizona Water Rights Settlement Act (SAWRSA). With necessary contracts signed in October 1983, the act became public law.

CHAPTER 12

SAWRSA and Tohono O'odham Preferences

Terms of the Act

In the settlement act, the Tohono O'odham are granted approximately 76,000 acre-feet of water a year from three different sources: 37,800 from the CAP; 10,000 from groundwater; and 28,200 from Tucson effluent. All water delivered to the reservation must be "suitable for agricultural use."

If the secretary of interior is unable to deliver the full amount of water, he or she must pay damages to the tribe depending on the type of water and on whether the CAP has been completed. If the secretary is unable to deliver the water, he or she must pay "the actual replacement costs" of the water incurred by the tribe if the CAP has not been completed.[1] If it has been completed, the secretary is obligated to pay "the value" of the water not delivered.[2] Under the act, the term "value" is "based on the tribe's anticipated or actual use of the water"[3] and is understood to mean the tribe will be compensated for lost jobs or farm income, not simply for the replacement costs of the water. Finally, if the secretary is unable to deliver the effluent or exchange water, he or she must also pay the replacement costs if a system to deliver the water is not completed in ten years, and the value of the water, defined similarly to the CAP case, if it has been completed.

Besides acquiring and delivering the water, the secretary must also "improve and extend" the irrigation systems on both San Xavier and Schuk Toak. The secretary is responsible for all operation and maintenance costs associated with the delivery of this water to the reservation. He or she must also establish a water management plan consistent with the Arizona Groundwater Management Act for San Xavier and Schuk Toak.

The secretary is required to carry out his or her obligations to the O'odham only if the tribe agrees to a number of conditions outlined in the settlement act. First, the tribe must agree to waive all past claims to water rights and to *injuries* to water rights within the Upper Santa Cruz Basin. Also, the tribe must waive all future claims to water in this basin. Both the tribal lawsuit and the suit of the allottees must be dropped, with prejudice.

Additionally, the tribe must agree to limit their groundwater pumping on San Xavier to ten thousand acre-feet of water a year and to the negligible amounts being withdrawn on January 1, 1981, on Schuk Toak. The tribe itself is responsible for developing the pumps necessary to utilize this groundwater. For the CAP water, the tribe has to subjugate the land at no cost to the United States and also assume responsibility for the operation and maintenance of the on-reservation works to be built by the secretary. The tribe also must use this water for agricultural purposes or else the Leavitt Act, a statute that defers construction costs on Indian irrigation projects, will not apply. Second, it is the sole responsibility of the tribe to design, construct, operate, and maintain the on-reservation irrigation system for any "exchange" water, water equivalent to the effluent water granted the tribe under the act.

Although the act grants the tribe the right to use the water received under the settlement for any purpose, including the leasing of water rights, other restrictions do limit its use. First, the tribe may not transfer water outside of the Tucson Active Management Area. This provision both limits the potential market for the water if the O'odham choose to lease it and prevents the tribe from delivering water to other parts of the reservation. Second, under the terms of the Leavitt Act, economic constraints may limit the use of water for purposes for which costs are not deferred as they are for agriculture. Third, because the tribe is responsible for the on-reservation irrigation system for the "exchange" or effluent water, it may not be economically attractive for them to use this water for agriculture. Instead, the exchange water may present the best, if not only, opportunity for leasing,[4] as is discussed more fully below.

To assist the tribe in the development of their water resources, the act provides for a $15 million Trust Fund. The O'odham may spend only the yearly interest and dividends. This money is to be spent for the subjugation of the land, the development of water resources, and the construction, operations, and maintenance of on-reservation facilities. An additional $3.5 million is authorized to assist the secretary in constructing the on-reservation system for the CAP water.

The act also sets up a Cooperative Fund to assist the secretary in carrying out his or her obligations. The fund is composed of $5.25 million contributed by the state of Arizona, the city of Tucson, and various mining and agricultural corporations, plus $5.25 million authorized by Congress, with a compounded ceiling of $16 million. Besides the costs associated with the construction and delivery of the water, this fund is supposed to cover damages. The secretary may spend only the interest that accrues, and only after the CAP is completed or after ten years from enactment, whichever occurs first. The act states that payments from the fund for damages may not exceed what is available in interest for any given year.

The Tohono O'odham certainly did not receive everything they requested. In fact, some of the provisions found in SAWRSA directly contradict their interests. They are the only water user in the state to have a firm limit on their groundwater use. The tribe was also required to waive past and future injuries to groundwater. Given the tailings ponds from the mines on the south side of the reservation, and the chemical contamination recently discovered in Tucson's wells, this waiver of damages associated with past water rights infringements may cause problems for the tribe if their water is found to be contaminated.

The tribe made a big concession when it agreed to postpone the delivery of water until the CAP comes on line in 1992. The tribe had requested the right to pump groundwater until the CAP water was delivered in full and to be allowed to pump recharge in order to fulfill their full entitlement. Neither of these requests are in SAWRSA. The tribe, although in immediate need of water for the farming operation, threatened by lack of water, could not have a new source of water for ten years.

The O'odham had to concede to accepting effluent water.

Throughout the negotiations, the O'odham had refused to accept effluent as part of their water supplies. Will Worthington, chair of the WRCC, urged the tribe to accept effluent exchange, an idea of Governor Bruce Babbitt, so that they could get the support of the state for the settlement. The act gives the secretary the power to exchange this water for other sources of water but only at his or her discretion. In a shortage year, the secretary will be competing with other interests and the city for all available water. Money, rather than water, may be all the tribe will receive from this provision.

Under SAWRSA, the O'odham also agreed to abide by a water management plan that "except as is necessary to be consistent with the provisions of this title, will have the same effect as any management plan developed under Arizona law" [sec. 303(3)].[5] This provision may bring the reservation's water use under state jurisdiction. The state has the authority under the Arizona Groundwater Management Act to require increasingly stringent standards with each planning period and to set water duties. These standards may require increased technology or low-water-use crops. The O'odham may incur higher costs for their farming operation because of these provisions.

The concession potentially most damaging to the tribe specifies that "payments for damages arising under 304(c) and 305(d) shall not exceed in any given year the amounts available for expenditure in any given year" [sec. 313(f)].[6] Although the tribal attorney argues that the accompanying conference report clarifies this phrase and allows the secretary to request additional sums, other interior officials have interpreted this clause as limiting the federal government's liability. Without doubt, there is not enough money in this fund to cover all the damages that would arise if the water is not delivered. The payment of damages is what will keep the implementation on schedule and consequently represents a large concession. For the Ak Chin Indians, the damages owed them is the primary force that has prevented their settlement from being completely neglected by the Interior Department.

The O'odham do have the promise that "wet" water will be delivered to the reservation or damages will be paid, and they have funds to develop the water. The tribe would probably not have gotten this promise or the money from the courts. But because the O'odham had few political resources, they had to enlist the support of the local interests in order to succeed in Congress. As a consequence, the tribe had to bargain, and sometimes give in, on many issues.

Some significant progress was made in terms of participation. Especially in the later stages of negotiations and especially in relation to the CAP, many decisions were made without much participation by the Tohonos. Though the Tohonos always held a veto power over negotiations, this power was limited because it could only be exercised if and when the terms of the settlement became very unacceptable to the tribe. The tribe did gain some expertise for future negotiations. Participation of the tribe in the bureaucratic arena during implementation can remedy some of the problems that have been noted in the act.

Tohono O'odham Preferences
for Water Resource Development

Sources of Information

What the Tohono O'odham decide to do with their water resources is subject to numerous constraints: physical and economic feasibility, the limitations placed in laws, the decisions of the secretary of interior, the vagaries of state and national politics, and of course, O'odham opinion or preference. Development projects, particularly water projects, are not likely to succeed without the active participation and support of the communities that they are designed to serve, and the O'odham are no exception.[7]

One reflection of O'odham opinion appeared in actions taken with regard to real-world political water rights negotiations. Another is available through opinion surveys. Here we review the results of two independent surveys of O'odham opinions about the major concerns of this case study, water and politics. It is important to note that individual opinions are subject to change through information and discussion. It is also important to note that there may be a difference between the tribal members' real behavior and what they may want ideally to exist. Finally, opinions and preferences are also tied to basic skills and information. A lack of information will act to limit the preferences and opinions expressed. The surveys represent opinions at one point in time during 1984.

The two surveys were conducted by different groups, on different parts of the reservation, using different sampling strategies. Where comparable questions were asked, however, the responses, in overall trend if not in statistical detail, are generally consistent. Generally, the few inconsistent results may be interpreted as differences in the nature of the two populations of Tohono O'odham interviewed, not as a result of differing survey methodologies. One exception to this conclusion will be discussed at some length—the high frequency of indeterminate answers ("I don't know") to questions posed directly to individual tribal members. Finally, it should be noted that there is one major difference between the two groups surveyed. One group, San Xavier, will receive water under the terms of SAWRSA, while those on the main reservation will not.

One of the surveys utilized a group interview technique.[8] At the request of districts on the main reservation, two researchers administered an open-ended questionnaire to district members at council meetings. Questions were asked to the group in attendance at the meetings, discussion ensued among the O'odham audience, and responses to the questions were then given. The methodology, unorthodox by the standards of survey research, sought to accommodate traditional modes of O'odham decision making. The responses recorded by the interviewers expressed the consensus of the community. That the group responses elicited by this procedure do not differ markedly from the individual statistical trends of a more common survey research approach suggests a rather close correspondence between the wishes of individuals and the consensus of the group.

Results of the second survey, conducted by the Bureau of Applied Research in Anthropology (BARA), are tabulated in the appendix to the "Socio-Cultural Impact Assessment of the San Xavier Planned Community."[9] The primary purpose of BARA's survey was to elicit the range of preferences for land use alternatives among members of the San Xavier District, as data for an evaluation of a large-scale lease proposal for that district. A total of 147 individuals were interviewed by a group of trained O'odham interviewers. The random sample was stratified by the variables of key interest to the impact assessment researchers: place of residence, and status of the individual as a shareholder in allotted land within the proposed lease site. Frequently, the results showed no statistically significant difference among the subsamples.

One result, of probabilistic significance at the .005 level, can be used to characterize the three subpopulations by place of residence. Tribal members living in the Tucson metropolitan area (23.3 percent of the total sample) use the O'odham language less at home than do their San Xavier (60.3 percent of sample) or main reservation (16.4 percent of sample) counterparts. Reflected in Table 12.1 is an "urban-rural continuum": if language use is a marker of assimilation, Tucson-area O'odham are more

Table 12.1. Tohono O'odham Language Use and Urbanization

Use of Tohono O'odham Language at Home	Place of Residence			Total
	Tucson	San Xavier	Main Reservation	
Always or mostly	19 (55.9%)	70 (79.5%)	21 (87.5%)	110
Seldom or never	15 (44.1%)	18 (20.5%)	3 (12.5%)	36
TOTAL	34	88	24	146
			[significant at .005 level]	

SOURCE: Adapted from BARA, 1984; Appendix B [see note (a), Table 9.1].

comfortable in the social patterns and values of non-Indian society than San Xavier residents. It should be noted, however, that in all three subsamples, O'odham language use predominates, and when a chi-square analysis was performed only on the San Xavier and main reservation residents, no statistically significant difference appeared.

We feel confident, therefore, that the sample drawn from San Xavier District members does not unduly err in the direction of assimilation. San Xavier District, by its proximity to metropolitan Tucson, is clearly at the forefront of political contests with non-Indian society. It was water from beneath that district's land that was at issue in the Southern Arizona Water Rights Settlement Act, and it is that district that is now most directly facing the question of putting expensive imported water to its "highest and best use." But the individuals of that district will confront these issues as relatively typical tribal members. Thus, in our efforts to interpret O'odham preferences for the future, we will lean more heavily on the results of the comprehensive BARA questionnaire, supplementing these results when appropriate with the findings of the community-level survey conducted by Vandemoer and Peters.

A major difference between the two surveys, as mentioned above, is the recording of indeterminate answers in the BARA questionnaire of San Xavier District members. In part, this is a methodological artifact. Surveys administered to individuals elicit that respondent's personal opinion. If administered carefully, the survey instrument does not demand that the respondent construct an opinion when in reality he or she has none. Group-level interviews elicit a group response. Individuals without a personal opinion within that group may be expected to defer to those who are more opinionated or more knowledgeable about the issues in question.

We suspect, however, that the large number of "don't know" responses from San Xavier District members reflects something more significant about political participation and efficacy. More so than the rest of the reservation, San Xavier District is faced with profound and imminent change. That many of the residents and members of the district appear to have indeterminate feelings about those changes is troublesome. They either lack adequate information to participate effectively in the process of deciding upon their future, or they are receiving overwhelming amounts of information. Analysis of results from the BARA survey seem to lend support to both of these interpretations.

Attitudes toward Water Use

In Tables 12.2 through 12.5, we have arrayed responses to questions on the preferred uses and sales of groundwater and surface water from the CAP, expected to arrive in the early 1990s. Several conclusions are immediately apparent. The preferred uses for groundwater, the only source of water now on the San Xavier Reservation, were for household consumption and agriculture. For CAP water, the "don't know" category replaced household usage as the second most frequent response, reflecting undoubtedly the lack of immediacy of this source of water, as well as unknowns such as the water's quality, timing of deliveries, and supply variations. Similar uncertainties appeared in response to queries on the sale of water. Only 6.3 percent of the respondents indicated a willingness to have groundwater sold; 19.0 percent sanctioned the sale of CAP water. Almost half of the respondents, however, simply did not

Table 12.2. Uses of Groundwater

"What do you think are the best uses of groundwater?"[a]	*Percentage of Respondents, Total Sample[b]*
Household uses	75.0
Agriculture	47.2
Don't know	6.3
Not concerned	0.7
Everything	0.7
For the Tohono O'odham	0.7
Recreation	0.7
Not for golf courses	0.7
For people who can't afford other water	0.7

SOURCE: Adapted from BARA, 1984: Appendix B [see note (a), Table 9.1].
[a]Multiple answers were possible.
[b]N = 142.

know whether CAP water should be sold. Some indicated a willingness to sell the new supply, if such sales generate income and assure enough water for use by the O'odham.

There is strong agreement, however, on the undesirability of selling groundwater. Over 75 percent of those responding were

Table 12.3. Sale of Groundwater

"What do you think about selling groundwater?"	Percentage of Respondents, Total Sample[a]
Don't want to sell	76.8
Need to save for future use	29.6
No specific explanation	28.2
Because it belongs to Tohono O'odham	12.7
Water not meant to be sold	2.8
Water is sacred	1.4
It is fresh	1.4
Tucson has its own water	0.7
Don't know	16.2
Do want to sell	6.3
Only if there is enough for Tohono O'odham	2.8
If price is right	2.1
No specific explanation	1.4

SOURCE: Adapted from BARA, 1984; Appendix B [see note (a), Table 9.1].
[a]N = 142.

Table 12.4. Uses of CAP Water

"What do you think are the best uses of CAP water?"[a]	Percentage of Respondents, Total Sample[b]
Agriculture	57.0
Don't know	32.4
Household uses (if treated)	18.9
Not good for household uses	4.2
Recreation	2.1
For the people	2.1
For reservation needs	1.4
To replenish groundwater	1.4
To reduce groundwater use	1.4
Not good for anything	0.7
Send to Sells (main reservation)	0.7
Trade for cleaner water	0.7
Not concerned	0.7

SOURCE: Adapted from BARA, 1984; Appendix B [see note (a), Table 9.1].
[a]Multiple answers were possible.
[b]N = 142.

Table 12.5. Sale of CAP Water

"What do you think about selling CAP water?"	Percentage of Respondents, Total Sample[a]
Don't know	50.7
Don't want to sell	26.8
Wasn't given to us to sell	21.8
Meant for farming	4.9
Do want to sell	19.0
To make money	11.3
If enough for Tohono O'odham	6.3
So they won't use our groundwater	0.7
Because it doesn't come from	
reservation	0.7

SOURCE: Adapted from BARA, 1984: Appendix B [see note (a), Table 9.1].
[a]N = 142.

reluctant to see groundwater sold, and those without such reservations wanted assurances that the price received was fair and that sufficient water remained for Indian use. Although the attitude is clear, the discrepancy between values and actions begins to show: for the San Xavier District is currently, in effect, transferring groundwater rights to the ASARCO copper operation.

Attitudes toward Farming and Alternative Land Uses

When questions of alternative land uses were posed to members of the San Xavier District (Table 12.6), less consensus emerged, and interesting differences, by place of residence of the respondents, became evident. San Xavier members living on the main reservation took a more preservationist attitude toward San Xavier lands, although their desire to "keep the land as it is" probably incorporated a feeling that the land is now being used primarily for farming and grazing. Among the other two subpopulations, there were fairly strong indications of polarization: significant numbers wanted the district left as it is; more wanted to see it developed for jobs and money. When the bottom half of Table 12.6 is examined, it is clear that some form of ranching and agriculture was the preferred mode of development for the majority of all respondents. Once again, however, uncertainty over the future was evident, particularly among those most directly affected by land use decisions at San Xavier. More than a third of the San Xavier resident subsample offered no clear opinion on how the district's lands should be developed.

Table 12.6. Attitudes Toward Future Land Uses by San Xavier District Members

	Percentage of Respondents by Place of Residence			
	San Xavier	Main Reservation	Tucson	Total Sample
"What is more important?"				
Develop land for jobs and money	47.1	25.0	47.1	43.4
Keep land as it is	33.3	54.2	41.2	38.6
Don't know	19.5	20.8	11.8	17.9
"How should land be developed?"				
Farms and ranches	56.5	78.3	76.5	64.8
Other than agriculture	7.1	4.3	11.8	7.8
Don't know	36.5	17.4	11.8	27.5

SOURCE: Adapted from BARA, 1984; Appendix B [see note (a), Table 9.1].

Table 12.7 reveals additional attitudes toward the preferred option of agriculture. The majority of respondents in the total sample did not or had not themselves worked in agriculture, yet considered farming a desirable occupation for future generations. This apparent discrepancy can be resolved by the facts that commercial agriculture is predominantly capital-intensive, not labor-intensive, that little subsistence-oriented, labor-intensive farming is now carried out on San Xavier, and by the overwhelming preference, noted in Table 12.7, that the O'odham themselves manage future agricultural developments on their reservation. The O'odham unable or unwilling to farm

Table 12.7. Attitudes Toward Agriculture among
San Xavier District Members

	Percentage of Respondents, Total Sample
"Have you ever considered a job in agriculture?"	
No[a] (Reasons given:)	62.4
Have no interest;	
Don't know how to farm;	
Too old, not well;	
Never thought about it.	
Yes[b] (Reasons given:)	37.6
Can grow your own food;	
Like that type of work;	
Like outdoors and animals;	
Have personal experience;	
That is my present job;	
Helps to reduce cost of food.	
"Do you want to see the younger generations working in agriculture?"	
Yes	61.5
No	11.9
Don't know	26.6
"Who should manage an agricultural development?"	
Tohono O'odham	86.8
Others	1.4
Don't know	11.8

SOURCE: Adapted from BARA, 1984; Appendix B [see note (a), Table 9.1].
[a]N = 91.
[b]N = 55.

now apparently see future generations of O'odham as potential managers of farms.

Attitudes toward Leasing Land to Non-Indians

Summarized in Tables 12.8 and 12.9 are Tohono O'odham attitudes toward leasing reservation land and toward non-O'odham taking up residence within San Xavier District. A consistent percentage of O'odham from the three subpopulations

Table 12.8. Willingness to Lease San Xavier Land

	Percentage of Respondents by Place of Residence			
	San Xavier	Main Reservation	Tucson	Total Sample
"How would you feel about leasing land to outsiders?"[a]				
Opposed	44.1	45.0	42.4	45.6
Not opposed	25.4	40.0	45.4	33.3
No answer	18.6	0.0	0.0	9.6
Don't know	11.9	15.0	12.1	11.4
"Have people offered to lease land from you?"[b]				
No	77.0	77.3	63.3	73.5
Yes	18.0	22.7	36.7	23.9
Refused to answer	4.9	0.0	0.0	2.7
"Would you live in a 'new town' on San Xavier?"[c]				
Yes	8.0	4.2	47.1	16.6
No	77.0	58.3	50.0	67.6
Don't know	14.9	37.5	2.9	15.9
"Who should manage the 'new town?'"[c]				
Tohono O'odham	66.2	65.2	83.9	70.2
Others	3.9	0.0	6.5	3.8
Don't know	29.9	34.8	9.7	26.0

SOURCE: Adapted from BARA, 1984: Appendix B [see note (a), Table 9.1].
[a]Asked of allottees only. N = 118.
[b]N = 118.
[c]N = 146.

surveyed were opposed to leasing, though this number did not represent a majority opinion. In the San Xavier resident sub-population, refusal and "don't know" answers formed a substantial portion of the variation. We suspect that these responses reflected a growing anxiety in individuals who would, by residential proximity to developments on leased land, be most directly affected. Currently, much of the allotted land on

San Xavier returns no income to its owners. Leasing offers to change this situation, but the long-term consequences may, to many tribal members, be difficult to accept.

Table 12.9, tabulating O'odham feelings toward non-O'odham residents on San Xavier, underlines the dilemma. A proposal made, but eventually not accepted, by the tribal council to construct a planned new community of more than one hundred thousand non-Indians would have generated income for individual allottees and district and tribal treasuries. Such a community would have contravened the attitude expressed strongly in Table 12.9 that non-O'odham should be allowed to live on O'odham lands only if they are either Indians from other tribes or are married to resident tribal members.

Table 12.9. Attitudes Toward Non-Tohono O'odham
            Living on San Xavier

"How do you feel about non-Tohono O'odham living on San Xavier Reservation?"	Percentage of Respondents, Total Sample
Opposed[a] (Reasons given:)	53.4
It's Tohono O'odham land;	
They'll take over our land;	
Because they're not Tohono O'odham;	
More will follow;	
No special reason;	
Teachings prohibit interracial marriage.	
Not opposed[b] (Reasons given:)	26.0
If they are married to a Tohono O'odham;	
Only if they are Indian;	
Only if they get district's permission.	
Don't know[c]	15.8
No response[d]	4.8

SOURCE: Adapted from BARA, 1984: Appendix B [see note (a), Table 9.1].
[a]N = 78.
[b]N = 38.
[c]N = 23.
[d]N = 7.

Political Participation and Efficacy

Despite a clear willingness to bear the costs of participating in decisions by attending meetings, the O'odham do not feel they have sufficient information to do so effectively. A third of the district's enrolled members (with, surprisingly, no significant difference by place of residence) are reported to attend district meetings, a major locus for the dissemination of information to the general tribal public. A similar percentage of the respondents claimed inadequate knowledge of the dominant issue then on the districts' agenda: the proposed new town. And over 70 percent felt they had been given inadequate time, as well as inadequate information, to fully evaluate the proposed lease. To an important extent, widespread and efficacious participation in decision making rests on time and knowledge. Inadequate supplies of both of these commodities may account for much of the anguish evidenced in the last tabulation of Table 12.10 Almost 80 percent of the individuals interviewed acknowledged intrafamily and intracommunity conflict over the major land use issue that confronts them. It is not surprising, therefore, that the tribal council eventually reversed a previous, more positive stand and informed the developer that the community lacked the time and information necessary to make a positive decision.

Summary: Preferences and Actions

Tohono O'odham preferences place some general boundaries around what water options may be favorably considered. Some boundaries are firmer than others. For instance, it is difficult to conceive of an option involving the sale of groundwater that would be readily embraced by the general populace of the O'odham were they given the chance to participate. At the same time, the substantial uncertainty about lease and sale of CAP water may mean that this alternative might be acceptable to the tribe with more information and time for consideration.

Table 12.10. Indicators of Political Participation
Among San Xavier District Members

	Percentage of Respondents, Total Sample
Do you attend San Xavier District meetings?"	
Yes	63.6
No	36.4
"Do you have adequate information on the proposed 'San Xavier Planned Community?'"	
Yes	20.3
No	68.4
Don't know	11.3
"Have you had adequate time to express your feelings on the proposed lease?"	
Yes	15.3
No	70.2
Don't know	14.5
"Have discussions of the proposed lease caused disruptions in the community?"	
Yes	79.7
No	1.5
Don't know	18.8

SOURCE: Adapted from BARA, 1984; Appendix B [see note (a), Table 9.1].

CHAPTER 13

TOHONO O'ODHAM OPPORTUNITIES
FOR RESOURCE USE

Introduction: Changes in the Regional Economy

The city, the mines, and the farms of the Tucson Basin were brought to task by the Tohono O'odham lawsuit for pumping too much water from under O'odham lands. These same elements of the regional economy will interact, in some ironic ways, in determining the future options of the tribe. The municipality continues to expand; indeed, the county is expected to grow by 630,000 new residents in thirty years. Tohono O'odham lands, especially those on the San Xavier Reservation, will experience intense pressures to absorb some of the growth, through residential or commercial leasing. The mines will play a rather different role in the future development of the reservation. Currently, copper underwrites a substantial portion of the tribal operations, through royalty payments from the ASARCO lease on San Xavier and the Noranda-Lakeshore mine on the main reservation. However, due to foreign competition, the future of the copper industry in the state is bleak. The O'odham will be forced to seek alternative sources of tribal revenues.

Agriculture, historically and currently the major consumer of water in the Tucson Basin, may likewise play an ironic role in the O'odham's future. The Arizona Groundwater Management Act of 1980, whose purpose is to bring the groundwater overdraft problem under control by 2020, will regulate agricultural water use progressively more strictly. These restrictions will not stop farming altogether in Pima County, but they may reduce cultivated acreage substantially. Although indirectly subject to the constraints of the state groundwater code, through the planning authority given the secretary of interior, the O'odham may yet find an increasingly viable economic niche: filling the vacuum created by the future decline in agricultural products in the region.

In this chapter we look at the possibility of using expected CAP water for agriculture on the reservation. And we examine the potential for putting water to "higher and better uses"—industrial, commercial, and residential development.

An Agricultural Future

The need for adequate planning of farming and grazing systems has long been acknowledged on the reservation. Participation of Indians in such endeavors, however, has not been extensive. Indeed, the consensus among observers of O'odham economic development efforts, whether in agriculture or in other economic sectors, is that lack of participation is a preeminent cause for failure.[1]

The efforts to introduce the *bolsa* farming technique to the Tohono O'odham Reservation is not an atypical example. Anthropologist Henry Dobyns, in his case study, "Blunders with *Bolsas*,"[2] recounts the extensive planning efforts by Indian agents during the 1930s. After touring *bolsa* farms in southern Sonora, Mexico, agents thought they had the answer to the precarious arroyo-mouth farming of the O'odham. *Bolsas* were, in essence, artificial catchment basins: earthen walls were constructed along washes to create a *bolsa* or pocket; after floodwaters from a single storm collected in the pockets and thoroughly soaked the soil, seeds would be planted.

The system proved a success on farms around coastal Huatabampo, Mexico, and agents for the Tohono O'odham had expectations that *bolsas* could turn the Indians into more efficient subsistence farmers. Several demonstration *bolsas* were constructed with the aid of the CCC in the late 1930s, including a series of connected basins, covering almost two hundred acres near the O'odham village of San Miguel. Employees from the agency's extension division operated the system and instructed local residents in the techniques. The system ran into immediate difficulty, however. *Bolsas* were built across the wash from the existing village. Three powerful O'odham cattle owners who controlled the area refused to allow additional land to be turned into homesites for the *bolsa* farmers. Moreover, the *bolsa* system required significantly more work than the traditional floodwater farming of the O'odham, and it required constant attention through the cycle of water catchment, land preparation, and cultivation. Yields turned out to be no better than the traditional methods, too, despite the increased labor demanded by the *bolsa*. Soon, the new system was rejected. Dobyns summarized the fundamental reason: "Administrators didn't bring San Miguel people into the preliminary planning of their *bolsa*. As one result, the project failed to fit into the current socio-cultural situation of the village in many respects. Since they did not participate in the planning enough to modify the project to fit their needs, San Miguel farmers have never felt it to be their own. To them, the *bolsa* remained government property—it put it there, it should make the *bolsa* work."[3]

Other efforts to enhance agricultural productivity on the O'odham reservation followed the aborted *bolsa* experiment. Results have been similar.[4] The San Xavier Cooperative Association, however, counters this general trend. Incorporated in 1971 by a group of allottees, the cooperative farm has demonstrated a potential for commercially successful agriculture. With a series of federal loans for land preparation and farm equipment, the organization has been able to cultivate up to one thousand acres of crops in any given year. Faulty managerial decisions have occasionally reduced yields, but the primary problem facing the San Xavier Cooperative Farm is an inadequate well capacity. Although sufficient water may be available in the underground aquifer, the tribe has lacked sufficient funds to construct, operate, and maintain pumps and wells. The cooperative thus illustrates the fundamental problem of commercial farming in arid and semiarid lands. Agricultural products may bring a good price on the market, but the water to grow these crops is not free. Water transport systems must be built to bring the water—whether from underground or from surface flows—to the farm. These systems are often technologically complex and expensive. Profit margins for all but the most highly valued crops, which are also the most risky to grow, will be low.

Economics of Farming

Expected deliveries of Central Arizona Project water to several districts of the Tohono O'odham Reservation in the early 1990s should enable tribal planners to begin again—to learn from past agricultural development efforts but to avoid the mistakes. Preeminent among these mistakes is the frequent reliance on outside "experts." But some more basic questions need to be addressed. *Can* CAP water be put to profitable use on an O'odham farm? Perhaps more important, *should* such a farming operation be expected to show a profit?

The wave of farm foreclosures throughout the country in the 1980s should modify our expectations. Caught between high production and capital costs and low market prices, farmers are experiencing troubled times. To expect tribal farm managers to avoid these difficulties is unrealistic. Inevitably, there will be years when a new Indian farm operation fails to cover the variable costs of operation, even if that operation employs state-of-the-art technology, has sufficient water, and makes the correct managerial decisions. Should losses become the rule, not the exception, there will be demands, from within the tribe and from water users throughout the Tucson Basin, to divert O'odham water to more efficient uses. Bank creditors will attempt to recover outstanding debts. Tribal officials will demand changes in management. In short, if the O'odham enter the farming business with unrealistic expectations, they will inherit the difficulties facing farmers throughout the country.

The alternative of subsistence farming may, however, be technologically infeasible, at least as far as CAP water is concerned. Historically, tribal members farming small plots at the mouths of arroyos relied on rainfall. The water was free, though they had to expend their own labor to divert the arroyo flows onto the fields. CAP water will require extensive and costly delivery systems. Many, but not all, of these delivery costs will be borne by the federal government, under the terms of SAWRSA. The O'odham hoping to divert their share of this new water to small, family-sized plots will be faced with the expense of an on-farm diversion system, the costs of land clearing and preparation, and the requisite capital and labor demands for yearly operations.

There is another impediment to small-scale subsistence farming with CAP water. Article 18 of the constitution revised in 1986 establishes, for the first time, a tribal water policy: "All waters originating in or flowing in, into or through the Tohono O'odham Nation, and all water stored in the Nation, whether found on the surface or underground, are a valuable public resource of the Nation to be protected for the present and future use of the Nation as a whole."[5] Recognizing the centrality of water as a resource, the policy statement empowers the Tohono O'odham Council to control and manage the resource "for the greatest public benefit." It is entirely possible that subsistence farming falls within the greatest public benefit. Certainly there is precedent for this in O'odham history. But districts on the arid main reservation may clamor for direct economic benefits from CAP water. Since it is technologically and legislatively prohibitive to divert water from the Tucson Aqueduct to remote western sections of the reservation, such benefits would have to come from revenue-generating uses of water in the Tucson Basin. Currently tribal policy holds that half of the income coming to a district for mineral leases or other economic developments be distributed to other districts. Through future decision by tribal officials, direct recipients of CAP waters in the eastern districts may be precluded from using the water for purposes that do not generate money.

Summary: Participating in Agricultural Decisions

Interested and competent experts blundered, according to Dobyns, when they attempted to introduce the *bolsa* system to the O'odham in the 1930s. Lest such well-intentioned failures be repeated in the 1980s or 1990s, when water from the Central

Arizona Project is delivered to the reservation, the tribe will have to participate fully and effectively in the important decisions to be made.

The major decision will concern the use of the imported water for agriculture. The Tohono O'odham have expressed preferences for such usage and have farmed historically, although the water has come from different sources. But farming is not the "highest and best use" of water in a semiarid but urbanizing region. Pressures will be brought to bear on the Indians to use their water supplies for other purposes, as discussed below.

Should water be put to use on farms, the decision then is whether to make farming operations serve the purpose of generating revenue or underwriting social goals, such as increased employment, family self-sufficiency, or a reinforcement of traditional lifestyles.

Should the tribe lean toward commercial farming operations, with the expectation that profits can be used to support development efforts elsewhere on the reservation, the crucial decision becomes, who will manage the enterprise? The leasing of agricultural land to outsiders is a dominant pattern on Indian reservations and has been actively encouraged by the BIA.[6] Non-Indian farmers often have the expertise in agribusiness that Indians lack; they absorb the risk of a commercial venture and absorb most of the profits as well. In the case of the Tohono O'odham Reservation, there are likely to be willing and competent outsiders poised to lease Indian land, as the existing farms in Pima County are placed under increasingly strict water-conservation requirements in the future. An equally prevalent arrangement is the non-Indian farm manager on an Indian farming enterprise. Often, the manager performs the function of a scapegoat, taking blame for lack of profits. Although such a role may deflect community conflict outward, it does little to increase the tribe's internal management capabilities. Before making such a management decision, the O'odham would do well to examine closely the experience of other Indian agricultural enterprises, for example those of the Navajo and Gila River tribes.

Given a free choice, the O'odham may choose to direct new

water supplies for nonagricultural uses. In that case, two potential opportunities present themselves: leasing of water to off-reservation users; and leasing of reservation land, accompanied by water, to non-Indians for residential, industrial, and commercial developments. We examine these options in the following sections.

The Leasing of Tohono O'odham Water Rights

During the negotiations preceding SAWRSA, one incentive extended to the O'odham was the right to lease their water for off-reservation use.[7] It was suggested to the O'odham that by selling their CAP water to local users, particularly the mines, they could raise the money needed to prepare new farmland.[8] Since under SAWRSA the Indian nation is responsible for the subjugation of the land, this option could prove to be a way to help finance this costly undertaking.

In addition, there was strong support among local water users for the O'odham to be able to lease their water.[9] Since O'odham claims were to be settled primarily with imported water via the Central Arizona Project, not groundwater, any CAP water allocated to the tribe meant an increased supply for all of Pima County. The O'odham water represented another source for the water-short county. As a result of this local pressure, the provision was included in SAWRSA that allows the O'odham to lease their water. Besides allowing the O'odham to put the water to any use on or off the reservation, SAWRSA also provides that

> the Papago Tribe may sell, exchange or temporarily dispose of water, but the tribe may not permanently alienate any water right. . . . such sale, exchange or temporary disposition shall be pursuant to a contract which has been accepted and ratified by a resolution of the Papago Tribal Council and approved and executed by the Secretary as agent and trustee for the tribe. . . . The net proceeds from any sale, exchange, or disposition of water by the Papago Tribe shall be used for social and economic programs, or for tribal administrative purposes which benefit the Papago tribe.[10]

This section, however, is no guarantee that the O'odham can lease their water; the determining factors will be the cost of the water and the demand in the marketplace. Unfortunately for the tribe, some provisions in SAWRSA affect the price the water could be sold for, and limit the potential market. As a result, the 28,200 acre-feet of "exchange water" present the best opportunity for sale.

Constraints on the Leasing of Water

In order to find a market for their water, the O'odham will have to set a competitive price, one that would entice local water users to buy tribal water as opposed to groundwater or CAP water. Under SAWRSA, the Indians are provided water from three different sources: groundwater, CAP water, and an additional 28,200 acre-feet of water "suitable for agricultural use." This last source of water, the "exchange water,"[11] will most likely be CAP water, but it is treated as a separate source because different provisions found in SAWRSA govern its use. Legally, the tribe may lease the water derived from all three of these sources and derive "net proceeds" from the sale. But as one writer noted, "Different cost factors will be associated with the transfer of each of these three types of water. The 'net proceeds' realized from the lease of Tohono water will vary depending upon the type of water involved and the use to which it is transferred."[12]

Under SAWRSA, the Tohono O'odham are limited to pumping only a little over ten thousand acre-feet of groundwater a year. This water could be leased, but first a large capital investment for new wells and a delivery system would be required. Although the tribe itself could finance the development of this water resource, it is more likely that the lessee of the water would cover the costs of pumping and transporting the water.[13] A number of other factors, however, make it unlikely that the O'odham will lease this source of water. One, the groundwater is the only source of water available to the tribe until the CAP comes on line, probably in 1991. Two, a lease executed in 1972 with ASARCO grants that mining company the right to pump sufficient water to process mined ores on the reservation.[14] ASARCO presently pumps approximately three thousand acre-feet a year but may pump up to five thousand acre-feet, approximately one-half of San Xavier's groundwater entitlement.

ASARCO's claim to the limited supply of groundwater will leave little water to lease.

Although legally the O'odham may also lease their CAP water, a number of provisions in SAWRSA encourage the use of this water for an on-reservation agricultural development. First, unless the tribe uses this water for agricultural purposes, construction costs associated with the delivery of this water will be charged to the Indians. The Leavitt Act, mentioned above, only applies "as long as such water is used for irrigation of Indian lands."[15] According to one legal analysis, the construction costs "will reduce Papago profits, but it will not necessarily make the water unmarketable because all non-Indians with CAP water allocations will have to pay some construction costs."[16] In addition, unlike other CAP allottees, no operation and maintenance charges will be assessed against the CAP allocation.[17] But a number of local water users are already balking at the price of CAP water,[18] and the assessment of construction costs may make the price too high for the market.

For the Tohono O'odham, the third source of water, the exchange water, "may represent their best opportunity for transfer."[19] Under SAWRSA, the secretary of interior is supplied by the city of Tucson with 28,200 acre-feet of effluent free of charge, and is instructed to deliver 23,000 acre-feet of water to San Xavier and 5,200 acre-feet of water to Schuk Toak. Although under the act this water could be the effluent itself, a provision that prohibits the secretary from constructing a separate delivery system to deliver reclaimed water makes it unlikely. Instead, other sources of water, including excess CAP water, are designated as substitutes for the effluent that the secretary is required to deliver to the reservation. Unlike the CAP water, there are no restrictions attached to the use of this water and no mention of the costs associated with the acquisition and delivery of the water, except that the secretary may use money from the Cooperative Fund to acquire and deliver the water.

Any discussion of the marketability of this water requires some speculation. As Nancy Laney observed: "A reasonable interpretation of the act's failure to specify costs for exchange water is that the water is to be given to the Papagos free and clear to do with as they choose. . . . The act deals with the Papagos' exchange water in an entirely different section than its regular CAP allocation. This seems to signify that exchange water is distinguishable from CAP water even if, in reality, both came from the same source."[20] In addition, unlike the CAP water, the O'odham are responsible for the "costs of design, construction, operation, and maintenance of on-reservation systems for the distribution" of this water.[21] This substantial expense would be avoided if the Indians leased this water.

Ultimately, it may be the secretary of interior in office at the time the Tohono O'odham wish to lease their water that will determine the marketability of O'odham water. The secretary will decide how costs are assessed in order to arrive at the "net proceeds from any sale, exchange or disposition of water."[22] The term "net proceeds" does imply some congressional intent that certain costs should be assessed against the water.[23] "Conceivably these costs could range from the barest amount necessary to cover direct administrative expenses in approving the contract to reimbursement for all related federal expenditures unless specifically exempted in the act."[24] In addition, the secretary must approve any contract that sells or exchanges the water. There are no standards provided in the act to govern the secretary's actions. Conflict between the secretary's reponsibilities as trustee and as head of a federal department with a taxpayer constituency could create problems. For example, if politically powerful interests do not like the Tohono O'odham's position as "water brokers," pressure could be applied on the secretary to negotiate a lease less favorable to the O'odham.

The Local Market

The market for O'odham water is restricted to eastern Pima County, or more specifically to the Tucson Active Management Area (TAMA). Reflecting the desires of local water users who wanted to keep as much water as possible in the basin, SAWRSA provides that all types of O'odham water may be transported only within the boundaries of the TAMA. This restriction of marketing to eastern Pima County will make O'odham water harder to sell. If this restriction were not placed on the potential market, the O'odham could have easily found a buyer for the water in Pinal or Maricopa County. Any water user located along the aqueduct could contract for the tribe's exchange water if CAP water were the water exchanged.

Three of the existing local users appear to be the most likely potential buyers: the mines, the city, and agricultural interests. Until the CAP contracts are signed, it is difficult to assess whether these users will want O'odham water. Citing the low quality and high cost of CAP water, many local water users have been shying away from signing CAP contracts. The Duval Corporation, Anamax, and Cyprus-Pima Mining Company have all stated that they will not purchase CAP water.[25] In 1985 other irrigation and mining enterprises were undecided. The city of Tucson intends to buy CAP water, but with the large purchases of farmland for its groundwater rights, the city appears to have as much water as it needs.

It is possible that if the Indians could offer their "exchange water" at a lower price than CAP water, they could find a market for their water among those users who cannot afford to contract for CAP water. Since industrial and municipal contractors must pay more for their water than agricultural users, a water company such as the Flowing Wells Irrigation District might be a potential buyer. As one official from this district noted, "A bargain always interests me," and if the O'odham can offer a bargain, they will have buyers.

New water users who will come into the Tucson area in the 1990s may offer another potential market. If most of the available CAP water is already contracted for, these buyers will be forced either to purchase water from the city or to buy up farmland and convert it to the appropriate type of water right required under state law. The head of the Tucson Active Management Area estimated that a new water user needing one thousand acre-feet of water will either have to pay the city at least $375,000 or spend almost $1,000,000 for water derived from farmland.[26] Perhaps such high costs will allow the O'odham to lease their water and make a nice profit.

Despite the uncertainties concerning tribal leasing of water, a number of factors are favorable. One, if the tribe can offer their exchange water at a lower price than CAP water, they will surely find a buyer somewhere in Pima County. Two, until the reservoir-storage system for the CAP is filled, many contractors for CAP water will probably not receive their full allotment. Since the O'odham enjoy a high priority, they may be able to sell their exchange water to fill this void. Three, if current negotiations between the Bureau of Reclamation and the Cortaro-Marana Irrigation District are successful, the secretary of interior will trade the 28,200 acre-feet of effluent for this district's CAP allotment. CAP water, as the source of the exchange water, will be the easiest to market: anyone along the aqueduct within TAMA could easily take delivery.

Leasing of water, if it occurs, will require substantial planning and negotiations by the O'odham with the Interior Department. Which costs will be assessed against the exchange water should be decided in a contract ahead of the time political pressure in the Tucson area might cause the secretary of interior to negotiate a lease unfavorable to the Indians. A number of Tucson water users do not fully accept that the O'odham can legally lease their water rights. Some interests feel that if the O'odham cannot use the water on the reservation, they should not get it, and will apply pressure on the Interior Department or local congressmen to restrict the leasing. Ill feelings may be somewhat negated by an attractive water price and good public relations. After all, it can be argued that Indians do not have access to traditional sources of financing and that leasing would help the tribe raise needed development funds.

The Leasing of Land

In 1983, a real estate developer from the Palm Springs area entered into negotiations with members of the San Xavier District Council to lease eighteen thousand acres of that district. Based on his experience in leasing Indian lands in Southern California, the developer saw a future potential for the district land. Urban Tucson, expanding rapidly through the 1970s and

1980s, is expected to grow even more dramatically by the end of the century. Land to absorb this residential, commercial, and industrial boom will be at a premium. By placing a large section of territory under long-term lease and laying the infrastructure for an entire "new town," the developer projected over one hundred thousand new residents for the San Xavier Reservation. The plan was ambitious, and it presented the Tohono O'odham a most difficult and meaningful choice.

Land leasing is not a new experience for the Bureau of Indian Affairs. Leases, in fact, have been a cornerstone of federal development policies for Indian reservations for decades. Before 1955, at the height of the termination era in federal Indian policy, leases were customarily granted only for periods of five to ten years. Under the threat of cancellation, short-term leasing was attractive only to farming and grazing operations. Legislation in 1955 extended the terms to twenty-five years. Motivating this extension was the belief that longer terms would attract more substantial financial investment toward reservation lands and resources. Since 1955, statutes, including one for San Xavier, have been written on a tribe-by-tribe basis to extend the maximum lease period to ninety-nine years.

Acting in its capacity as manager of tribal nonallotted lands at San Xavier, the district council signed a complex lease agreement with the developer in August 1983. By signing, the council committed 3,400 acres of tribal land to a proposed new town and seemingly opened the way for the developer to sign individual lease agreements with owners of 15,300 acres of allotted land. Two overriding concerns pushed the district council to its decision. Revenues to support social, educational, and economic programs on the reservation were in jeopardy. To fund a variety of ongoing programs, tribal officials were relying on royalty payments from two copper operations on reservation land and on the monies apportioned to Indians in the federal budget. Copper prices had fallen, as had the income accruing to the O'odham from the mining leases. Simultaneously, federal funding for Indian programs had been reduced substantially, a decrease of 22 percent between 1982 and 1983.[27] Like reservation leaders throughout the West, O'odham officials were desperately searching for new sources of revenue.

Equally salient to San Xavier councilmen was the realization that allottees could negotiate to rent, or even sell, their parcels to outsiders. An unwritten rule of community consensus that alienation of land was wrong had previously been enforced by peer pressure. The consensus was weakening in the face of attractive outside propaganda benefiting individuals. At the same time, fractionation of allotment parcels through nearly a century set the context for individual "nondecisions" regarding the disposition of property. In a general review of the heirship problem on Indian reservations, Ethel Williams noted the consequences: "When the number of heirs becomes so large that the return to each heir is minimal, all are disinterested in managing their land."[28]

The fear of the alternative induced the San Xavier District Council to listen seriously to the proposal for an eighteen-thousand-acre lease. The council was afraid that the land would be leased out and carved up "piecemeal," that owners of individual allotments would rent to unsavory leasees for unacceptable purposes. The district would thus develop in an unplanned, uncoordinated manner. The Palm Springs proposal seemed to offer in contrast a fully planned new community, with controls over what could be built and where it could be built.

Political opposition quickly arose to the district council's decision. Criticism ranged from lack of community participation in the council's actions to the potential loss of newly gained water rights to the development. The council's decision appeared to have been made with some haste—for fear, as noted above, that the area would be developed piecemeal. And the water rights of the planned new town were, at this point, entirely unspecified. These rights awaited a "master water plan," not yet written.

The overarching fear among the opponents to the lease concerned long-range loss of control over San Xavier to the non-Indians of the proposed new town. The lease contained some provisions for O'odham supervision of non-O'odham and for tribal administration of the governmental affairs in the development. But at a volatile public hearing on the proposed lease late in 1983, the concerns expressed by the dissidents were broader than the simple mechanics of town administration. They were concerned that their potential influence on the key decisions of larger political arenas—in the Tucson Basin, the state, and at the national level—would be completely lost. Politicians making choices on matters affecting San Xavier would be quick to listen to a constituency of one hundred thousand non-Indians on the reservation, and slow to respond to the one thousand or so O'odham there.

Opponents of the land lease achieved a victory in the O'odham tribal council. Although the development corporation had obtained approximately four hundred signatures of allottees, representing about thirteen thousand acres of the planned eighteen thousand acres, the council voted against the lease after a long meeting attended by over one hundred opponents of the lease.[29] The council voted 18–4 in approving a motion to overturn the San Xavier District council's previous approval of the lease.[30] The motion overturned the district's approval of the lease "unless and until the terms have been renegotiated with the tribe and allottees in a fair and equitable manner and to negotiate directly with the people involved including the tribe, tribal entities, allottees and not just with the Bureau of Indian Affairs."[31] Although not an outright rejection of the development itself, the tribal council's vote was certainly a rejection of the proposed lease and a serious setback for the developer.

The eighteen members of the tribal council evidently were expressing the views of constituents in rejecting the lease. In May 1985, residents of San Xavier voted out of office four of the five district council members who had been principal supporters of the lease.[32] Four opponents of the lease, including the president of the antidevelopment Defenders of the O'odham Land Rights Inc., were elected to the council in their place. As a result, opponents of the development held four of the eleven district seats on the council, although they failed to capture the office of district chairman. With two more votes, the district council could reverse itself and cancel the lease altogether, as well as pass zoning laws that would effectively block large-scale residential development.

The Santa Cruz properties lease is only the first of many proposals that probably will be received by the Tohono O'odham as non-Indians begin to recognize the worth of the water received under the settlement. The controversy over this proposal holds many potentially useful lessons. The development repeated the mistakes of the past by being conceived and planned with little Indian participation, and hence was opposed by many O'odham. As one Indian at the May 1985 tribal council meeting noted: "They've [developers] been talking for six years already. This was the first time our people had to talk."[33] Whether the Santa Cruz proposal eventually goes forward, or whether others later suggested will be accepted, will depend upon openness and communication.

Opportunity and the Burden of Choice

Water per se is not the key to Tohono O'odham economic development, but put to use wisely water may bring substantial economic benefits. More importantly, successful decision making about water may build the sense of community and confidence in collective decision-making processes. However, with opportunities come the burden of making choices. The new water to be made available by SAWRSA introduces the possibilities for various agricultural development plans, the sale and/or lease of water, and the lease of land for agricultural, residential, or commercial development. The successful implementation of any of these options will require resources, some of them in short supply for the O'odham. Depending upon the option, capital, skill in management, and the ability to negotiate shrewdly will be necessary. The O'odham themselves are the best judges of both their goals and their resources.

CHAPTER 14

STRATEGIES FOR THE FUTURE

SAWRSA and the Control of Water

The Southern Arizona Water Rights Settlement Act (SAWRSA) represents the first opportunity the Tohono O'odham have had to control their water resources in many years. Throughout most of their history, the O'odham relied primarily on rainwater and limited surface water on San Xavier for their water needs. It was therefore when the O'odham gathered collectively to sing and pray for rain that they felt in control of their water destiny. The notion that people could influence a meteorological event through prayer and ritual strikes many contemporary desert dwellers as preposterous. Yet to traditional O'odham who "sing rather than pump" water onto their fields,[1] rainwater remains a precious and dependable source of water. It is a water supply that the O'odham feel they can control without large amounts of capital and equipment.

This sense of efficacy persists among some O'odham today. As one Catholic member noted, "I still believe in Jesus and the saints, but I know too that when we drink the wine and sing for I'itoi's help, the rains always come."[2] Another farmer, waiting for the rains to soak his field, remarked, "You got to know the right old songs—Then you got to dance to bring down that rain."[3] But for many other tribal members, who endured years of government policies, making it difficult to pursue the traditional life, this sense of efficacy is gone. Rain, they believe, comes less frequently.[4] The BIA is primarily responsible for developing the water supply for the reservation, and so most O'odham feel powerless to control their water resources. The Settlement Act comes as a real opportunity for Tohonos to reassert control over water and related economic development.

There is both hope and controversy on the Tohono O'odham Reservation concerning the settlement act. To most O'odham, "water is precious, it's a very special gift."[5] Some find it is difficult to talk of selling water or of its "best" economic use. Water is a "sacred thing" and "sales and people clash with sacred things."[6] Yet the reservation is plagued with high unemployment rates. The water provided under the settlement act promises to bring with it opportunities to exercise power and to progress economically. As Hilda Manuel, a tribal member, explained, "I think water to us means survival. . . . Any chance or any hope any of us have for becoming self-sufficient goes out the window if we can't depend on our main source of life, our water."[7]

In the near future, the Tohono O'odham will make substantive choices regarding both their land and water. These choices have the potential to enhance the quality of life on the reservation and to increase social well-being. They also may enlarge O'odham control over their resources and their future. For this potential to be realized, attention must be given not simply to the engineering details of these decisions but to the opportunities to enlarge tribal participation in internal and external arenas.

Internal Politics

The Tohono O'odham are now confronted with a reservation system and decision-making structure not of their own design. Where decisions used to be made through deliberation among members of the family and the village, they now are made through the representative government of the councils and through the bureaucratic processes of tribal and federal agencies. Where dialect groups used to be autonomous but symbiotic, the district organization has, to a significant extent, rigidified this former flexibility of movement and interaction. Where land once was communally owned and used, now, at San Xavier, much of the land is allotted to individuals.

Although these changes are the legacies of external decisions, the resulting problems can, and should, be addressed only by the O'odham themselves. The constitution ratified in 1986 provides a new and improved decision-making machinery. Through that governmental mechanism a number of water-related issues will need to be addressed.

Foremost is the equitable distribution of rights and benefits. New surface water supplies will reach only those districts touching the Tucson Basin and the Tucson Aqueduct. But the moral and political weight of the Tohono O'odham Nation as a whole helped to shape the settlement of the tribe's water claims. The benefits that accrue from the use of this new water can partially underwrite development projects elsewhere on the reservation. Procedures will have to be established for distributing these potential revenues and, more importantly, for identifying the uses to which these revenues can most effectively be put. This will require an enhanced flow of information. District officials will need to know what magnitude of revenues they can reasonably expect to receive. Tribal planners will need to know the real wishes and necessities of the districts. And, within the districts, these needs and desires may be difficult to articulate without increased information. This appears to be the lesson that San Xavier District must learn. Confronted with a land leasing proposal of almost overwhelming complexity, the typical response was "I don't know." District-wide consensus cannot be founded upon such degrees of uncertainty.

The San Xavier Reservation itself faces some more peculiar internal problems, again not of their own making. Federal directives of a hundred years ago caused the land there to be allotted to individual tribal members, and the recent legislative settlement of San Xavier's water claims avoided the issue of what rights those allottees have to water. The tribe has chosen the direction it will pursue—water is a public resource, not appurtenant to the land of the individual allottees and their heirs. This policy should be implemented in a manner acceptable to the O'odham themselves. It will undoubtedly find resistance among those non-Indians who seek to lease and develop the lands of those allottees.

Substantive Choices

By defining new and existing water supplies as public resources, the water policy of the new O'odham constitution empowers the tribe to decide how these supplies can be most
beneficially used. Future options on water uses will be heavily
constrained by the external political and economic environment, however. Land values, market conditions, and power
relations in this larger environment are constantly changing.
Nonetheless, it is possible to identify some promising
strategies.

Preeminently, the water promised by SAWRSA must be put
to use. In arid and semiarid regions, paper water rights do not
directly translate into wet water. Rivers in the Southwest have
seldom fulfilled the demands of all those holding legal rights
to their flows. The Central Arizona Project will be no different.
The combination of expected water shortages and overalloca-
tions will fortify the old truism, "Use it or lose it." If the O'odham
do not have the structures in place—whether they be canals
for irrigation or treatment plants for domestic water deliveries—they may face intense pressure to forfeit their rights.

Putting water to use does not mean that the Tohono O'odham
should commit all their promised water to large-scale, irreversible uses. Long-term leasing of land for residential, commercial, and industrial development could be one such irreversible
commitment. Although the O'odham would retain proprietorship over their lands and earn income under long-term leases,
they would also foreclose their future options on that land.
Perhaps for this reason, as well as lack of information, the
tribal council decided to postpone indefinitely any positive decision on the San Xavier planned community proposal.[8]

Devoting all available water to agriculture would likewise
foreclose future choice. Reserving some water for leasing would
provide more flexibility. Should municipal users in the Tucson
Basin demand, and be able to pay for, some of the O'odham
allocation, they will require potable water. The tribe can plan

now for this eventuality by obtaining space in municipal water treatment facilities or constructing on-reservation plants.

The logical approach for the Tohono O'odham in water planning is to seek the greatest flexibility and diversity. A strong Indian preference has been shown for agriculture. However, specific and detailed analysis should undergird actual decisions. Market conditions for vegetables and traditional field crops should be projected. Soils need to be analyzed. Appropriate management structures must be designed, and personnel must be adequately trained. Crop mixes should be selected so that the risks inherent in farming are reduced and the economic viability of the operation is enhanced. The O'odham must anticipate inevitable errors in judgment by their farm managers and unpredictable shifts in weather and markets; but non-Indian farms are no less prone to these problems.

Whereas diversified cropping patterns can ameliorate some of these uncertainties, flexibility of water use can guard against others. When consumer demand for agricultural products is satiated, the treatment and sale of water may be more profitable. When acreage farmed by non-Indians in the Tucson Basin declines, under the increasingly strict conservation requirements derived from Arizona Groundwater Management Act, the expansion of O'odham agriculture may be a logical step. When non-Indian farmers face short-term cutbacks in the expected supply of water from the Tucson Aqueduct, the O'odham may find temporary and profitable markets for their own allocations. To retain flexibility in the use of their water supplies, they must be wary of binding commitments, both to their own agricultural operation and to potential municipal and other purchases.

Protection of the remaining O'odham groundwater supplies is imperative. This battle will have to be fought in the external arena. Mines are already threatening the quality of the aquifer; municipal pumping will continue to threaten the quantity of this supply. The O'odham agreed in SAWRSA to a cap on their yearly pumping rights. Now, they will need to assure those rights are economically available and not degraded.

The External
Environment

The Tohono O'odham cannot have a successful water strategy without involvement in the external political arena. It is in this arena that the tribe may influence to their advantage the interpretation of ambiguities in the settlement act. The office of the secretary of interior will determine the water management plan and the conditions under which O'odham water can be leased. Decision-making arenas external to the tribe will make numerous key decisions concerning the CAP in the next ten years that will affect the O'odham.

There are two facets of increased O'odham participation in the external political arena—one positive, the other involving costs. The exercise of O'odham influence builds a sense of both individual efficacy and community well-being. Participation can enhance feelings of control over external events. At the same time, participation takes resources. It demands time and energy for consensus building and conflict resolution. Certain skills are essential for effective participation in certain arenas. For instance, legal skills are necessary to pursue O'odham interests in the courts. The federal establishment is a byzantine and confusing world that requires political sophistication to manipulate successfully. Water development is a highly technical subject that requires some engineering expertise for effective participation.

At the present, the Tohono O'odham may lack some of the requisite resources for participation. It may not be possible to develop skills for every arena at one time, and it will be necessary to choose where to specialize. It is important to note that participation without adequate resources may be dangerous. If the results of decision making do not serve O'odham interests, the tribe may simply lend legitimacy to decision making by nominally participating without getting anything in return. Even so, we believe they must actively attempt to influence the external environment. With or without their participation, crucial decisions are to be made that will deeply affect them.

Although lacking traditional political resources, the tribe does have some resources that will be of use in the external arena. First, they own seventy-six thousand acre-feet of water a year. As Tucson continues to grow, the tribe's water will only increase in value as new water users will require a dependable supply. Second, the Tohono O'odham enjoy a unique legal status as an Indian tribe. Largely exempt from state jurisdiction, the tribe is in a strong position for future negotiations. They can use this special status as a government to distinguish themselves from other groups in the Tucson area. Third, the O'odham can threaten to and actually withhold their participation in selected situations. They have the power to lend legitimacy to decision-making processes. By withholding their participation and stating why, the O'odham may command some influence. Finally, the tribe can always utilize the federal courts to enforce provisions in the settlement act.

Cultural misunderstanding and intolerance is a limitation on Tohono O'odham participation that possibly may be mitigated. The reservation runs on a different timetable than the outside world, requiring long periods of time to build a consensus on major decisions. One pressure the O'odham have always faced, and will continue to face, is the speed with which decisions are demanded by the non-Indian world. In addition, many misconceptions exist about the O'odham, especially in terms of employment. The general public, and elected officials, could be educated into greater understanding and tolerance in a number of ways. Many writers have written extensively about O'odham culture.[9] Also, funding obtained from humanities and historic groups could be used to build cultural exhibits and promote tours of the reservation.[10]

By acknowledging the costs as well as the benefits of participation, and by marshalling the resources available to it, the Tohono O'odham Nation can become an effective actor in the external political environment. Decisions within three levels of this external environment will require the tribe's attention over the next decade.

Local, State, and National Arenas

With their participation on the Water Resources Coordinating Committee (WRCC), the O'odham established an important precedent. It was the first time the tribe had had some influence, however limited, over local water use decisions. By continuing its membership on the committee and on other local groups, and increasing its level of participation, the tribe can increase its influence in the basin. It can also benefit from increased contacts with the city of Tucson, which, along with the O'odham, is the largest contractor for CAP water.

Most of the Tohono O'odham's interaction with the state of Arizona will be through the Tucson Active Management Area (TAMA) Office. This office is responsible for implementing the provisions of the Arizona Groundwater Management Act. Although lacking direct enforcement powers over Indians, TAMA officials promulgate the basin-wide conservation measures required by the management act. Mandated to achieve a "safe-yield" in the basin by 2025, TAMA will be monitoring regional groundwater. Some water users in the basin have suggested "dewatering" certain areas in the basin such as Avra Valley, while trying to achieve a balance in other areas. Increased pumping in these relatively rural areas would affect the reservation's groundwater tables. Negotiating with the TAMA office to protect its groundwater could thus have substantive benefits for the tribe.

The implementation of the Southern Arizona Water Rights Settlement Act will require increased O'odham participation at the federal level. Two separate federal bureaus, the Bureau of Reclamation and the Bureau of Indian Affairs, have responsibilities under the act and previous legislation. The secretary of interior, as trustee for Indian lands, guarantor of the provisions of the settlement act, and supervisor of both the BIA and the Bureau of Reclamation, has wide discretion over the tribe's future. The Tohono O'odham would do well to seek access to the decision-making process directly in the secretary's office.

In the inevitable negotiations to resolve ambiguities in SAWRSA, the tribe should not lose sight of its status as a semisovereign government within the federal system. The O'odham can utilize their "government-to-government" relationship to gain the ready contact with Washington decision makers that lobbyists for special interests groups must cultivate over years of effort. This contact will not guarantee decisions favorable to the O'odham, but it will assure that their interests are heard.

The Internal Political Environment

Political gains in the external environment may lead to political losses at home, in the internal environment of the Tohono O'odham Reservation. One of the major tasks facing tribal leaders and their constituents is to accommodate two different modes of decision making. Historically, decisions made by the O'odham reflected the consensus of the community. Key decisions made in the non-Indian arena are typically made by those to whom authority has been delegated by their constituents. The clash between consensus and delegation is not a new one for the O'odham—its roots lie in their uneasy previous acceptance of the Indian Reorganization Act. At that time, elected O'odham officials had to make unpopular decisions on stock reduction. Now, tribal officials have made decisions on issues of water supply and usage that have not been fully acceptable to their constituents. These conflicts will continue, as O'odham leaders participate in the decision processes of the external environment, and as tribal members seek to participate in decisions made on the reservation.

Throughout much of the preceding analysis of Tohono O'odham history, politics, and economics, two elements shoulder the blame for unacceptable decisions and unworkable solutions—lack of time and lack of information. Decisions made in the external arena, commonly by actors who covet O'odham resources, have been made hastily. Asked to participate or respond to these decisions, the O'odham have seldom had the time necessary to work through their traditional consensus-building processes. Lack of information is a corollary to this accelerated pace of decision making. Seldom have the expected consequences of programs and policies been fully understood. Seldom have tribal members acquired the knowledge to understand, and thus evaluate, alternatives.

Although we suggest that the Tohono O'odham continue to participate in the political processes of the external environment, we also recommend that, as a condition for their participation, they insist upon adequate time and information. By doing so, O'odham leaders and their constituents are more likely to be satisfied with the results of the choices to be made. It is interesting to note in this regard that the O'odham tribal council took this exact stance in regard to the San Xavier Planned Community. Reversing a previous, more favorable council vote, the tribal representatives have effectively required the developer to restart the proposal process at the beginning.[11]

CHAPTER 15

Differences and Similarities between the Tohono O'odham and Upper Rio Grande Hispanics

Introduction

On the surface it would seem that a world of differences separate the experience of the Hispanics in the Upper Rio Grande and the Tohono O'odham in southern Arizona. Racially and culturally the two have little in common. The homelands of the two groups are separated by hundreds of miles and provide dissimilar resource bases and climates. Hispanics live in high mountainous terrain fed by numerous snow-fed streams, with harsh winters and cool summers. The O'odham are desert dwellers, dependent until recently on intermittent rains and pumped groundwater. Their seasons vary from warm to scorching.

Beneath the marked dissimilarities between the two groups of people, however, lie commonalities important to our theme. Both are poor rural minorities, and water resources offer them some opportunity for the future. The intent of this chapter is to distill from among the obvious differences the common threads that link the experiences with water of these two groups. It seems reasonable to suppose that whatever conclusions and lessons can be drawn from our study of these disparate groups may well have wider application among poor rural peoples elsewhere.

Some Important Differences

It is important to recall at the outset of this comparison the differences in extent to which Hispanics in the Upper Rio Grande and the Tohono O'odham actually control water resources. Long tenure in residence permits both groups to be thought of as natives, although the hundreds of years of Hispanic occupation is far shorter than the very long experience of the desert dwellers. Perhaps because they had more of it, the Hispanics' management of water achieved greater technical complexity and grander scale. No doubt survival on the desert required understanding of harsh, hydrologic realities and careful husbanding of water resources, but water conveyance and distribution required less construction and less complex rules. Hispanics, though increasingly pressed, have been better able to maintain water management structures and organization. Their *acequia* system persists. In the case of the O'odham, on the other hand, the widespread practice of desert agriculture with surface water has lapsed. Pumping groundwater has been an Anglo technology introduced to the O'odham, and a technology they have never themselves controlled. Unlike the Hispanics who run their own irrigation systems, the O'odham were generally dependent on the Bureau of Indian Affairs to provide wells and on the federal government to protect water beneath their lands from exploitation by others. Whereas the Hispanics are concerned with maintaining control over water, the Tohono O'odham struggle, with some recent success, to gain control.

Not only do Hispanics have greater control over water resources than do the O'odham; as individuals, Hispanics have greater control over other conditions that influence their lives. Both populations have high unemployment and underemployment, but the job situation is clearly worse for the O'odham. Those Indians who work for pay, a distinct minority, are most often dependent on government jobs. For the most part, the plight of the O'odham community is the general plight of the Indian in our society. Indians have a great deal at stake in the Washington connection—with the BIA and other federal agency and congressional actors. The individual Hispanic is a good deal more autonomous. Hispanics may have two jobs, one of part-time farming of their own land and the other full- or part-time elsewhere. Although Hispanics take seriously the task of maintaining their shared culture, they are also fiercely individualistic. They have a strong sense of ownership of their own land and their own water and they make their own choices. The O'odham are more comfortable as a collective. They tend to be egalitarian to the extent that they downplay their differences. Standing above or outside the group is considered unseemly, and there is subtle social pressure to defer to the consensus.

Although there are many similarities between O'odham and Hispanic relations with the dominant culture, which are discussed further below, generally Hispanics appear to have exercised greater community control. Much of O'odham experience with water management in this century has simply been a pattern of deferring to outsiders about water projects on Indian lands. In the cases of both the *bolsa* experiment and the Tat Momolikat Dam, projects that turned out to have no benefits for the Indians were imposed from outside. Although a number of crucial water decisions have been made in the Upper Rio Grande without taking Hispanic interests into account, Hispanics were able to defeat both the Taos and the Llano projects, which were largely sponsored from outside and failed to get Hispanic support.

The extent to which the two communities have been involved in negotiation rather than litigation to settle disputes also distinguishes the O'odham from the rural Hispanics. Although the Indians used a court suit to bring the dominant interests to the bargaining table, the Southern Arizona Water Rights Settlement Act was pounded out through a long process of negotiation, both in southern Arizona and in Congress. Water rights in the Upper Rio Grande are still embroiled in a major court suit that has pitted Hispanics against Indians. The conflictual litigation appears to be taking a heavy toll in terms of time, money, and good will, and our discussion has suggested that greater openness to negotiation would be advisable. At the same time we should note once again that the negotiation strategy of the O'odham has depended on the great stake that non-O'odham water users have had in coming to settlement, and that the *Aamodt* litigation in the Upper Rio Grande was not initiated by either Hispanics or Pueblo Indians.

More Important Similarities

Although it is highly unlikely that either Hispanics or Tohono O'odham have much knowledge about or interest in each other's problems and situations, there are sufficient commonalities of experience that each would seem to have much to learn from the other. Both are minorities imbedded in an aggressive, dominant society with little understanding of cultural differences. As minorities, both groups cling to their historic lifestyles and culture. They maintain separate and flourishing languages, distinct from that of the dominant culture. Neither wishes assimilation with mainstream America, although each desires more material well-being. Residents want to stay where they are, and for the most part resent the intrusion of outsiders. Both feel that their separateness and culture are under siege.

Both the Upper Rio Grande Hispanics and the O'odham are agrarian people, and both face impediments to sustained agriculture. Some partitioning of land into small plots has occurred in both places, partially through inheritance practice in the Upper Rio Grande and government allotment programs for the O'odham. These small units make it difficult to achieve economies of scale in production or marketing. Further, there is a shortage of the trained labor required for intensive agriculture. The time for Hispanics is divided between their farms and part-time jobs. Even more serious, a high percentage of O'odham are not engaged in agriculture at all at present. Problems of gaining sufficient capital to farm and finding dependable markets differ in extent, but not in kind.

Given an opportunity to express preferences, both the Hispanics and the O'odham prefer to allocate water to agriculture rather than to other uses. In the case of the Hispanics, agriculture provides a means for maintaining much of their current culture and lifestyle. For the O'odham, agriculture is clearly preferable to other alternatives that threaten the invasion of non-Indian peoples into O'odham lands. In both cases, although agriculture involves considerable risks, there is at least the opportunity through agriculture to achieve improved economic returns. More analysis of details is necessary, but it appears that growing higher-value crops in both areas is feasible.

The most meaningful and interesting similarities between the Hispanics in the Upper Rio Grande and the Tohono O'odham in southern Arizona appear in the nature of their participation in important water resources decisions affecting them. Our interview data indicate that neither the O'odham nor Hispanics feels that they have much influence over, or are well represented in, decisions made at the state and the federal level. Neither group has had much impact upon setting the timing and agenda of water decisions. Broad legislative mandates that establish the terms under which water decisions are considered, such as the San Juan–Chama Diversion or the Central Arizona Project, were made largely without the effective participation of these poor, rural, minority groups, despite their considerable interest at stake.

Often, matters directly affecting these groups, such as the adjudication of water rights in northern New Mexico or most pre-lawsuit decisions on the Tohono O'odham Reservation, occurred on a timetable that generally accommodated others more than these minorities. Along with the minimal influence over the timing of decisions closely affecting their interests, these groups have also lacked influence over how questions were framed and the alternatives to be considered. In the case of the Hispanics, water development proposals were cast in ways that conflicted with their cultural institutions rather than harmonized with them. As for the O'odham, little opportunity to salvage their declining water table presented itself, even though theirs was the oldest and best legal claim to groundwater. The O'odham have settled for Central Arizona Project water and municipal effluent, even though the delivery and sale of such water involves technical and political complexities that the community might well have preferred to avoid.

Neither the Hispanics nor the O'odham have felt that they had the necessary resources to participate effectively in decisions. Lack of information is a common complaint. Although it turned out that the *Aamodt* court case was to affect them directly, Hispanics were for a long time ignorant of its implications. The high percentage of O'odham responding "I don't know" to our questions about legislative settlements and proposed leases attests to their lack of information or tools with which to assess information. In the *Aamodt* case, Hispanics have felt the lack of legal expertise that was provided to their adversaries. Although the O'odham had effective representation in bringing the water suit that gave them leverage in the legislative settlement, their sources of information were narrow, often restricted to only their legal counsel, upon whom they were highly dependent. Further, the tribe has lacked independent, hydrologic expertise and advice, even though they must act in a political arena where expertise carries much weight and most of the contending interests are well supplied with such expertise.

Neither the Hispanics nor the O'odham has yet to achieve a high degree of active participation in water resource decisions. Especially in the case of the O'odham, there was a time when decisions were made without even formal and ceremonial voice. Today, this minimal participation is no longer acceptable to these rural minorities. Responding to initiatives taken by others represents somewhat greater participation and both the O'odham and Hispanics know how to flex this kind of muscle. Hispanics have defeated unwanted water projects. The O'odham initiated a court suit in response to Anglos' mining of groundwater resources. Full participation, however, involves being able to articulate the community's own independent values, even when they are at odds with the values of the dominant society, and to have them be included in the water agenda. The prevailing pattern has been to label as backward and hopelessly unmodern concerns outside the dominant development coalition in water. Issues are framed and alternatives set out without the perspectives and values of the rural poor being incorporated or balanced with others. Instead, when minorities have been accommodated at all, it is largely at the margin, after other, more dominant interests are satisfied, and within a definition of progress that is aimed toward goals to which the rural poor do not unqualifiedly subscribe.

Other aspects of the decision-making processes have inadequately provided for participation on the part of the rural poor. Pressure to decide has come before these communities have had a full opportunity to consult with one another concerning their preferences. The arenas in which choices are made are often geographically distant from the area where poor rural people live. Important meetings are seldom held in remote villages or on the reservation. The language spoken by decision makers is usually alien. Often the rural poor have had to petition through the courts for access to decisions. The judiciary has a long-standing commitment to see that insular minorities, whose interests might otherwise be poorly represented, have a hearing. Undoubtedly, the poor would be less well off without judicial intervention.

At the same time, appeals through the courts have limitations. It is expensive to buy legal representation. Talented youth that move into law forego some other occupation that might provide other needed expertise, and their youth are the most valuable resource of these communities. Other groups may have superior legal talent and better access to other participants in the litigation process. Moreover, it is important to recall the discussion in Chapter 2 concerning the shifting emphasis within the judiciary toward the commodity viewpoint. The courts probably will not be the friend to the rural poor that they have been in the past.

The skills and criteria being applied in natural resource decision making also work against full representation of the values of the poor. Natural resource decisions are heavily dominated by expertise from engineering, the physical sciences, and economics. This kind of knowledge is more likely to be held by the powerful than by the rural poor. The recent emphasis on water as a commodity has highlighted the economic value of water, including the benefits and costs of allocating water to highest uses. Yet this strict commodity perspective fails to include the community views of water held by the rural poor.

Highest Use of Water and the Rural Poor

The first imperative in using water resources, according to both our Hispanic and Tohono O'odham informants, is to serve community values and to maintain culture. Increasingly in the larger society, the highest use of water resources is measured in terms of an economic calculus, weighing economic benefits against costs. Yet both groups of rural poor express in words, and some actions, a willingness to forego maximizing economic returns from water allocation in order to pursue activities compatible with culture and lifestyle. In particular, both the Hispanics in northern New Mexico and the O'odham in southern Arizona prefer to use their water resources in irrigated agriculture rather than other uses, even if potentially more profitable. Both groups are opposed to uses that might introduce into their midst numbers of newcomers who do not share their heritage. Both groups are also opposed to the sale of water. Hispanics are also opposed to water leasing, though the O'odham show some uncertainty about leasing the newly acquired water, particularly municipal effluent. Our conclusion, based on interviews and the recent record of events, is that these two groups of rural poor see the principal value of water as something other than its highest economic use.

Material improvement is important to both Hispanics and the O'odham. But they want it to occur through the maintenance of their cultural identity rather than at the expense of it. Although some may reject the commodity value altogether, for many it is the affirmation of community values that is important. Economic betterment must be accomplished within the framework of satisfied community values. This perspective will be increasingly tested in the years to come.

Comparative Agricultural Strategies

In the case of both the Hispanics and the Tohono O'odham, our analysis shows that the allocation of water to the agricultural production of high-value crops could result in an improved economic return. Although agriculture might not be the highest economic use of water, and although agriculture entails certain risks, using water in agriculture could result in economic improvement for Hispanics and the O'odham in a manner consistent with their cultural concerns. The problems with an agricultural strategy are substantial for both groups, and they are largely social in character rather than of natural origin. But beyond these basic similarities, the differences predominate.

For the O'odham, an agricultural strategy implies large-scale, corporate-style farming. For Hispanics, in contrast, the strategy requires marketing and production associations of relatively small, individual farms and ranches. In terms of experience in farm management, both are short in terms of the crops that would bring greater returns, but many Hispanics at least have been operating farms on a part-time basis for many years. The O'odham, on the other hand, will have to acquire the needed skills during the years preceding the arrival of CAP water. From a marketing perspective, the O'odham have the advantages of existing wholesale outlets and the prospect of sufficient volume to allow a successful marketing operation. For Hispanics, the organizing of marketing associations is in itself one of the major tasks they face.

Some, though not all, of the capital needed to develop the tribal irrigation system is at least authorized by the settlement act, though that fact in itself does not guarantee appropriation. Hispanics are as yet critically short of the water storage facilities and diversion structures necessary to successfully grow higher-valued crops. Water is under different ownership in the two situations. Community ownership is the norm for the O'odham, whereas Hispanic water rights are held individually. Organizational differences correspond to the pattern of water rights ownership. The O'odham have a collective government with authority to make agricultural decisions. Hispanics, even with their community *acequias*, have no collective organization for making non-water-related decisions. Although the latter arrangement allows for more individual latitude and initiative, it also makes more difficult the job of organizing production and marketing operations.

For both the Tohono O'odham and Hispanics, the implementation of an agricultural strategy is a formidable task. Yet the strong attachment to water and culture in each case provides a motivational force of substantial magnitude as revealed in both opinion and action.

CHAPTER 16

Water: Opportunity and Challenge

The Meaning of Water

We began this account of water and poverty in the Southwest with two questions. How is water important to the rural poor of the region? What realistic, water-based strategies offer the best hope for improving their general welfare? This concluding chapter returns to these questions, starting with a general summary of what we have learned about the meaning and importance of water.

The meaning of water in the West is changing. According to many observers of water policy in the West, a new era of water management is dawning in which water is increasingly recognized as an economic commodity.[1] Instead of simply building new sources of supply to meet increasing water demands, states and cities will reallocate water from lower- to higher-value uses. In some areas, markets will play an increasing role in facilitating these transfers, and generally throughout the region higher prices for water will promote water conservation and greater efficiency in water use.[2]

However, along with this change, certain constants concerning how people feel about water will remain. A basic tenet of this book is that water has an emotional and symbolic meaning for the West that transcends its commodity value. In an arid region water is a fundamental resource, closely bound up with community survival and opportunity. Water was often woven into the mythos of prehistoric Indian peoples. The long-term settlement of Spanish conquerors depended upon the construction of water supply and irrigation systems. Water also had an important role for the Anglos who came later. Ever since the scientific explorations and writing of the visionary and creative geographer John Wesley Powell in the last half of the nineteenth century, water has been viewed as the key to the development of the West. For over a hundred years it has fueled the imagination and sustained the effort of countless individuals and groups who have successfully worked long and hard for this hydrologic dam or that reclamation project. Even today, the language used by political leaders and journalists in reference to water is often emotional and symbolic.

Critics of past water policy have believed that the emotional and symbolic ways in which people have regarded water have lead to water policies that are insensitive to environmental and economic implications of actions. Dams and reservoirs have been built that drown lovely canyons and destroy scarce riparian habitat. Further, the nation as a whole has been made to pay for water projects of dubious economic merit and that in any case benefit but one section of the country. There is no question that in the emerging era of water resource management, the environmental implications and commodity value of water will and should be given greater weight. Yet having experienced the negative consequences of disregarding the commodity value of water, it would compound past error to embrace now a narrow and exclusive view of water that ignores its community value.

Whether or not the community value of water is explicitly recognized as the motivation, there is little question that such concern will continue to be reflected in the water policies pursued by the dominant Anglo society. The desire for security and control over water has long been held more important than efficient water allocation. Although people are increasingly sensitive to efficiency, they are not likely to abandon water completely to the vagaries of markets that might introduce insecurity. Instead, markets are likely to be constrained by governmental policies aimed at protecting state and local control over the resource. Historically, politically desirable water projects were clothed in the fig leaf of economic respectability through the application of benefit-cost analysis. In the new era of water management, the economic evaluation of water pro-posals will perhaps be less manipulated and will be more in-fluential. So long as community values are not at risk, it may be economic rather than emotional concerns that are articu-lated in Anglo water politics.

A central aim of this book has been to specify explicitly and to reassert the community value of water so that the interests of low-income people can have greater credibility in the new management era. In Chapters 2 and 3 we point out that water has always been closely associated with security, opportunity, fairness, participation, and protection of the resource. Comfort-able that these values are being served in their communities, Anglo water policy makers are turning toward improving water efficiency. The two case studies of the Upper Rio Grande His-panics and the southern Arizona Tohono O'odham demonstrate that for poor rural people, however, community values associ-ated with water are far from secure. The rural poor's preoccu-pation with the symbolic and emotional meaning of water may appear to some to be backward and outmoded in the new, more economically conscious context. We have argued, however, that the desire of the rural poor to preserve the community value of water is not unique in western society. It appears to be different largely because the community aspirations they hold in regard to water, unlike most of the dominant culture, have not been satisfied.

The community value of water far outstrips its commodity value among poor rural people. Such sentiments must not be dismissed as "woolly headed" or "impractical." It must be re-membered that these people were largely left out of the water development decisions that secured others' demands for con-trol and security over water. When poor rural people sense a threat to their water rights, they feel their culture is at stake. Recalling once again the words of Judge Art Encinias in decid-ing against a proposed water transfer in northern New Mexico: "The deep felt tradition-bound ties of northern New Mexico families to the land and water are central to the maintenance of that culture. While these questions seem, at first, far removed from the simple question of the transfer of a few acre feet of water, the evidence discloses a distinct pattern of destruction of the local culture by development which begins with small, seemingly insignificant steps."[3]

Water, Poverty, and Participation

Realistic, water-based development strategies for the poor must rest upon a clear understanding of the link between poverty and water. It is easy to come to false conclusions founded solely upon economic reasoning. Poverty, defined in economic terms, largely means low per capita income. Since the rural poor use water mainly for low-value uses, whether water is lost or gained would not appear to much affect per capita income levels. Yet a powerful but subtle relationship exists.

Poverty is more than low income and has roots outside economic processes. When we initiated our description of the rural poor in Chapter 1 with economic indicators, we acknowledged that poverty had a more profound, political definition, that is, the lack of effective influence over important decisions affecting their lives. People are impoverished when they lack influence over such an important substance as water. Participation was identified as a key community value associated with water in Chapter 3. Participation in water resource decisions, therefore, becomes a vehicle for the alleviation of poverty, which promises to extend beyond whatever income may be generated by putting water to work in economically profitable activities.

The case studies of the Upper Rio Grande Hispanics and the Tohono O'odham of southern Arizona teach that the barriers against the participation of the rural poor in water resources decisions have been truly formidable. John Gaventa in his study of rural Appalachia described means by which power is brought to bear against effective participation of the poor.[4] According to the type of power employed by the dominant interests, participation by the poor ranges from limited to nonexistent. Our case studies have also provided a full array of examples.

Participation by the rural poor in water resources decisions has been prevented by structural barriers. The relationship of Indian tribes with the federal government has often in the past constituted a wall between Indians and participation. As federal wards, Indians have been excluded from state and local decision making. Failure of the federal government to fulfill trust responsibilities left Indian interests unrepresented. Lack of control over land and water resources locked Indian people out of development opportunities that were pursued by their Anglo neighbors.

Lack of the necessary political resources to make their case has limited the efficacy of poor people's participation when it has occurred. Under some circumstances the powerlessness of the poor has rendered their participation merely ceremonial. In other cases they have had some influence, but only the sort that can be used to prevent. Upper Rio Grande Hispanics have not been very successful until recently in securing help for development projects that would protect and improve their ancient community irrigation systems. In examples we have cited, however, they have exercised veto power over potentially damaging projects that they perceived would serve only the interests of others.

The principal circumstances under which participation by the poor has positively served their interests occurred in our case studies when they coincided with other more-powerful Anglo interests. The relatively weak power position of the Tohono O'odham in negotiating a settlement through Congress made necessary an alliance with Anglos, whose goals and interests were much more fully served in the eventual settlement than were those of the O'odham. In the Southern Arizona Water Rights Settlement Act, the O'odham participated substantively but only within an agenda set by others.

Manipulating the way in which questions are raised and which interests are considered is the most subtle and in many ways the most formidable barrier to full participation by the poor in issues affecting their lives. Policy actions taken under such circumstances are simply unresponsive to the aspirations, wants, and needs of people because they never get articulated and never appear relevant to the issues on the table. Such manipulation induces alienation, quiescence, and ineffectiveness in the poor, which often appear on the surface to be the cause rather than the result of inadequate participation.

Participation is distinct from the question of winning or losing. Although it is almost certain that purely nominal participants will lose, it is not true that participants must win to be effective. The real question is the degree to which their interests are accepted by other participants, and whether issues are seriously addressed that are responsive to those interests. We cannot draw a precise boundary between fully effective and ineffective participation, but we have identified the direction in which the potential process must move in order to become more participatory. Water-based development strategies must be consistent with the preferences of the Upper Rio Grande Hispanics and Tohono O'odham themselves and must be paths to which they are willing to marshall and commit their own resources.

Water and Opportunity

The way in which an issue like water is perceived structures or elicits the public response it receives. Because water is a highly emotional issue closely bound up with ideas of community, self-determination, and survival, it prompts a committed, group response that is a necessary ingredient to successful economic development. The literature on economic development identifies commitment, organization, and participation of the poor themselves as the key necessary ingredients.[5] Water, therefore, offers empowerment.

There are indications that the Tohono O'odham and Upper Rio Grande Hispanics have already begun to take control of water decisions affecting their lives. The impetus for participation was defensive. Faced with a declining water table that was killing trees and drying up wells, the O'odham filed suit against most water users in the Tucson Basin. Confronted with development projects that they perceived to be injurious to both their economic condition and to their culture, Hispanics defeated the Indian Camp and Llano projects. What began as defensive strategies have taken a more aggressive turn. The O'odham chose to participate in the basin-wide negotiations leading to the Southern Arizona Water Rights Settlement Act. The Hispanics have politically engineered funds for the construction of concrete diversion structures in the Rio Grande to serve the same *acequias* that opposed the Llano project.

Whether water can serve as the means through which community cohesion and organization can be forged has yet to be proven. Additional skills and even more perseverance than has already been demonstrated will be required. Can the O'odham make the agreement reached actually produce the benefits it contains? Water accords reached by the Ak Chin, Gila River, and Navajo tribes have not produced the agreed-upon benefits within the timetable originally set. Hispanics continue to be concerned over the security of their rights rising from the *Aamodt* and related suits, as well as from market pressure as addressed in the Encinias opinion. They have evidenced considerable political skill in achieving their objectives. Can they extend their capacity and deal effectively with clashes in the courtroom and marketplace as well?

Successfully coping with external forces is only the beginning. It is easier to mobilize a community against a common external threat than to build internal discipline and organization to pursue a collectively set goal. Learning to successfully operate a large agricultural enterprise as the O'odham intend is a major undertaking. A balance must be struck between the internal political need to distribute benefits and the necessity of businesslike efficiency to succeed in the marketplace. The decentralized, frequently small, private landholdings of part-time Hispanic farmers make it equally difficult for them to achieve the organized marketing requisite for successful agricultural redevelopment.

Is it fair to ask whether, despite the litany of pressures and problems, opportunity for improved welfare exists? Four factors underlie our positive, though qualified, response.

First, both Hispanics and Indians have a strong and extensive claim on an increasingly valuable natural resource within
the Southwest. Hispanics in the Upper Rio Grande hold and
exercise substantial quantities of water rights. The "paper
rights" of tribes, though short of control over "wet water," are
proving to be substantial levers in the legal and political arenas.
The O'odham have shown that both water and capital can be
produced if the desires of Indian rightholders are compatible
with the water agenda of the dominant culture.

Second, there are enhanced opportunities during a time of
major institutional and policy change to seize benefits even if
unintended. The public welfare criteria governing transfer of
water rights recently enacted by the New Mexico legislature[6]
came about through pressures having nothing to do with the
preservation of Hispanic culture in the northern part of the
state. Yet the criteria provide an opportunity to Hispanics that
has already benefited them in one court case.[7] Similarly, the
desire for leverage to insure completion of the Tucson Aquaduct
despite changing national water policy provided a fortuitous
opportunity for the Tohono O'odham.

Third, the changing nature of the water decision process in
the West, coupled with the arrival of a new generation of water
officials, results in more receptivity to new ideas and a wider
array of interests. Through opening up water decision-making
processes and broadening power, ideas that may have been
vetoed by a single water authority can have new life. New leadership is frequently less encumbered with the "old baggage" of
the past and is more receptive to new possibilities.

Fourth, the growing vigor, determination, and skill with
which the interests of both Hispanics and Indians are asserted
provide, in the final analysis, the most important determinants
of success. The cadre of young Indian attorneys produced in
recent decades has not only strengthened the efficacy with
which the Indian interest is argued in courts of law but has
spread their influence into finance, politics, and elsewhere.

Water is likely to be only one instrument to improve the welfare of the rural poor in the Southwest. This book has focused

exclusively on the relationship between water and poverty in the region and has not examined the full range of community development issues. There may be other ways for communities of Hispanics and Indians in the Southwest to acquire the cohesion, organization, motivation, experience, and necessary skills to effectively compete and assert their developmental interests within the dominant society. We argue that water offers an important opportunity and that failure here may make more general success impossible.

A General Strategy: The Challenge

There is a tendency among those who have long battled in the trenches to achieve economical and social betterment for the rural poor to become cynical about supposed opportunity. To such persons the water-based development strategies we identified at the end of each of our case studies may appear hopelessly naive. The counterarguments are easy to anticipate.

Some feel that in light of the long-term regional decline in irrigated agriculture, it is foolish to suggest that the rural poor base their programs for economic progress upon agriculture. Yet we have provided solid interview evidence that both the Tohono O'odham and Hispanics hold a strong preference for agricultural development. At bottom, unless the development strategy is in accord with community values, the chances for success are slim. Even though impediments to economically profitable farming operations exist, the case studies suggest that using water for high-value crops is feasible. Further, with a growing population and the prospective decline of other agriculture in the region, markets may open up for successful Indian and Hispanic enterprises.

Others may feel that the organizing capability of poor rural Hispanics and Indians to mobilize effectively in order to secure water and put it to economically beneficial use is so debilitated that attempts at real change are practically hopeless. Such an attitude, we think, ignores clear evidence that poor rural people have already been subjected to unrewarding challenges far more trying and risky than the ones we suggest and have survived with a surprisingly strong sense of community and identity. We believe that human resourcefulness is a renewing reservoir that ought not to be underestimated.

Some critics may hold the bitter opinion that the rural poor will always be kept poor and that they will never be allowed by the dominant culture to fully participate in water resources decisions. It is true that in the past the poor have generally not been included, and even when allowed to participate they have not had sufficient resources to protect their interests. However, such a view ignores the very real improvements in the degree of participation that has been achieved in recent years. Instead of being utterly absent from decision-making arenas, the rural poor have wielded some power, as we have documented. It is still true that the poor have not yet been able to frame water issues in ways that are responsive to their needs. Yet it would be incorrect to dismiss past progress or to predict that somehow the future holds certain reversal. There are too many examples in American life of poor ethnic minorities that once were powerless and now have influence to suggest the persistence of a stable oligopoly in water resource decision making. There are reasons why dominating interests may now be willing to share power. The development period in water resources was plagued by persistent perceptions of injustice. Currently, divisive and time-consuming conflicts are threatening the social harmony. If such future costs are to be avoided, the rural poor must be brought into the management coalition.

Finally, there may be those who feel that the activist strategies we have suggested for the rural poor are simply too risky. It is argued that merely agreeing to come to the bargaining table invites defeats of real significance. The poor, so it goes, usually lose in negotiations and so have actually contributed to their loss by even being present. For some it may appear preferable to remain apart from results so that it is clear that agreements were imposed rather than bargained. Although involvement in water politics has risks and success is not guaranteed, exercise of control over water resources is enormously important to community well-being. The costs of not exercising control are certain to be very great. This is a time of change, and the water institutions and policies being shaped now will govern western water affairs for decades to come. The challenge is to make these new institutions and policies responsive to the rural poor, and it has two sides. On the one hand, the rural poor must accept the reality of the new management era in water and the more stringent requirements on water use it imposes. But society as a whole must accept the validity of the Hispanic and Indian values and find ways to accommodate them. We conclude that both dimensions of this challenge can be met, though meeting them will take concerted and sustained effort.

NOTES

1. WATER AND THE RURAL POOR
IN THE SOUTHWEST: AN OVERVIEW

1. Although subject to various geographical definitions, as used in this book the Southwest loosely refers to the Four Corners states of Colorado, Utah, Arizona, and New Mexico.

2. Philip L. Fradkin, *A River No More: The Colorado River and the West* (Tucson: University of Arizona Press, 1984), 155. Much the same point is made even more strongly in Donald Worster, *Rivers of Empire: Water, Aridity, and the Growth of the American West* (New York: Pantheon Books, 1985).

3. See, generally, Norris Hundley, jr., *Water and the West: The Colorado River Compact and the Politics of Water in the American West* (Berkeley: University of California Press, 1975); and Norris Hundley, Jr., *Dividing the Waters: A Century of Controversy between the United States and Mexico* (Berkeley: University of California Press, 1966).

4. *Winters v. United States*, 207 U.S. 564 (1908).

5. Article VII, Colorado River Compact, Nov. 24, 1922, Santa Fe, New Mexico.

6. Many of the facilities that have been built, for example, El Vado and Abiquiu dams, were designed as either flood protection or storage facilities to serve municipal and agricultural interests lower in the basin.

7. "While the San Juan-Chama Diversion and the Navajo Indian Irrigation Project were authorized together, congressional appropriations for NIIP lagged far behind. By 1970, the SJD was 65% complete while NIIP was only 17 percent constructed." Charles DuMars, Helen Ingram, Ronald Little, Bahe Billy, and Phil Reno, "The Navajo Irrigation Project: A Study of Legal, Political, and Cultural Conflict," in *Water and Agriculture in the Western U.S.: Conservation, Reallocation, and Markets*, ed. Gary D. Weatherford (Boulder, Colo.: Westview Press, 1982), 110.

8. Speech to the Western Governors Association, May 22, 1984, in Palm Springs, California.

9. This theme of regional transition from water development to water management is not new [see, for example, Gary D. Weatherford, ed., *Water and Agriculture in the Western U.S.: Conservation, Reallocation, and Markets* (Boulder, Colo.: Westview Press, 1982)]. Yet it is not well understood outside of the West, nor is its fundamental character always fathomed in the West itself. Its validity, however, is a basic

premise of this book even though the book focuses only on certain equity aspects of it.

10. The dam was Indian Camp Dam, which was accompanied by a proposed Taos Conservancy District. See John Nichols, "Land and Water Problems in Northern New Mexico" (Paper presented at the University of New Mexico School of Law, October 16, 1975).

11. *New Mexico v. Aamodt*, 537 F. 20 1102 (10th Cir. 1976).

12. See Chapter 6 below.

13. For the United States as a whole in the 1980 Census, 13 percent of the population had income below the poverty level.

14. The mean score for all U.S. counties is zero. For further definition of the indices, see the National Institute on Alcohol Abuse and Alcoholism, *County Alcohol Problem Indicators 1975–1977* (Rockville, Md.: Public Health Services, U.S. Department of Health and Human Services).

15. Bureau of the Census, "General Population Characteristics," in *1980 Census of Population*, Table 55—State Summaries (Washington, D.C.: U.S. Department of Commerce, 1980).

16. For a description of Indian movement along New Spain's northern frontier from the sixteenth through the nineteenth centuries, see Albert Schroeder, "Shifting Survival in the Spanish Southwest," in *New Spain's Northern Frontier*, ed. David Weber (Albuquerque: University of New Mexico Press, 1979), 237–255.

17. See, generally, Michael C. Meyer, *Water in the Hispanic Southwest: A Social and Legal History, 1550–1850* (Tucson: University of Arizona Press, 1984); also Charles T. DuMars, Marilyn O'Leary, and Albert E. Utton, *Pueblo Indian Water Rights: Struggle for a Precious Resource* (Tucson: University of Arizona Press, 1984).

18. See note 17 above.

19. See, generally, Wells A. Hutchins, *Water Rights in the Nineteen Western States*, vol. I (Washington, D.C.: U.S. Government Printing Office, 1971), 159–175. The territorial legislature of New Mexico recognized prior appropriation in 1851; Colorado, in 1861; Arizona, in 1864; and Utah, in 1881.

20. *Winters v. United States*, 207 U.S. 564 (1908).

21. *Arizona v. California*, 373 U.S. 546 (1963).

22. For a survey of recent Indian water disputes, see John A. Folk-Williams, *What Indian Water Means to the West* (Santa Fe, N.M.: Western Network, 1982).

2. THE RISING COMMODITY VALUE OF WATER AND IMPLICATIONS FOR THE RURAL POOR

1. See Bureau of the Census, *Census of Population—Number of Inhabitants, United States Summary* (Washington, D.C.: U.S. Department of Commerce, April 1983).

2. Examples of municipalities that purchase water rights whenever they are available are Albuquerque and Farmington, New Mexico. The city of Albuquerque has set aside a special fund to purchase water rights and has a standing offer for purchase of rights (Fred Muniz, City of Albuquerque Water Department, personal communication, December 1984). The city of Farmington has a standing offer to purchase water rights and occasionally places an ad in the newspaper. Water right purchases under this policy have not been large, but there has been a steady volume of small purchases (Chuck Giles, city of Farmington, personal communication, December 1984).

3. Hoover Dam and the All-American Canal (to Imperial Irrigation District) were authorized by the Boulder Canyon Project Act of 1928. Glen Canyon Dam, in the southern tip of the Upper Colorado River Basin, was authorized in 1956 by the Colorado River Storage Project Act. This latter act also authorized other dams and diversion works in the Upper Colorado River Basin including portions of the Central Utah Project, which diverts water from tributaries of the Colorado into the Great Basin. For the story of some of these dams and diversions, see Norris Hundley, Jr., "The West against Itself: The Colorado River— An Institutional History," in *New Courses for the Colorado River*, ed. Gary D. Weatherford and F. Lee Brown (Albuquerque: University of New Mexico Press, 1986).

4. For a brief discussion of the Carter "hit list" and other Carter water policies, see Dean Mann, "Institutional Framework for Agricultural Water Conservation and Reallocation in the West: A Policy Analysis," in *Water and Agriculture in the Western U.S.: Conservation, Reallocation, and Markets*, ed. Gary D. Weatherford (Boulder, Colo.: Westview Press, 1982), 10–11.

5. For discussion of this point see Rebecca Roberts and Lisa Butler, "The Sunbelt Phenomenon: Causes of Growth," in *The Future of the Sunbelt*, ed. Steven Bullard and Thomas James (New York: Praeger Publishers, 1983).

6. For a paper that covers water right transfers in some basins of New Mexico, Utah, and Colorado, see F. Lee Brown, Brian McDonald, John Tysseling, and Charles DuMars, "Water Reallocation, Market Proficiency, and Conflicting Social Values," in *Water and Agriculture in the Western U.S.: Conservation, Reallocation, and Markets*, ed. Gary D. Weatherford (Boulder, Colo.: Westview Press, 1982). For discussion of water transfers in Utah, see John Keith, K. S. Turner, S. Padrinchas, and R. Narayinan, *The Impact of Energy Resource Development on Water Resource Allocation* (Logan: Utah Water Research Laboratory, 1978). Additional discussion on water transfers in Utah is in Ronald Little and Thomas Greider, *Water Transfers from Agriculture to Industry*, Institute for Social Science Research on Natural Resources (Logan: Utah State University, June 1983). For additional information on water transfers in New Mexico, see Rahman Khoshakhlagh, F. Lee

Brown and Charles DuMars, *Forecasting Future Market Values of Water Rights in New Mexico*, Report 092 (Las Cruces, N.M.: Water Resources Research Institute, 1977).

7. See Rahman Khoshakhlagh, F. Lee Brown, and Charles DuMars, *Forecasting Future Market Values*. For water rights prices in the San Juan Basin, see Table 5.9, p. 104. For prices in the Santa Fe area, see Table 5.6, p. 102.

8. This is a quotation from the 1982 opinion in the *El Paso* case; see U.S. District Court for the District of New Mexico, *The City of El Paso v. S.E. Reynolds*, Civ. No. 80-730 HB, January 17, 1983. See also Tim De Young, Manuel Avalos, Jay W. Pozenel, and Scott V. Nystrom, *Preferences for Managing New Mexico Water*, Technical Completion Report, Project 13457 (Las Cruces, N.M.: Water Resources Research Institute, 1984).

9. An example of the participation of District farmers in the opposition to El Paso pumping is the meeting held at the Elephant Butte Irrigation District office in August 1983. See "Water Lobby Group Launches Informational Effort on Suit," *Albuquerque Journal*, Aug. 30, 1983.

10. This conclusion, as well as many others in this chapter, cannot be tightly analyzed here without devoting a disproportionate amount of space to these context chapters. For supporting analysis, see Gilbert Bonem, "The Economic Importance of Water" (John Muir Institute and University of New Mexico, May 1983). See also some of the articles cited by Bonem: Keith et al., *Energy Resource Development*, 1978; Charles Howe and Douglass Orr, "Effects of Agricultural Acreage Reduction on Water Availability and Salinity in the Upper Colorado River Basin," *Water Resources Research* (October 1974); M. Gisser, R. Lansford, W. Borman, B. Creel, and M. Evans, "Water Trade-Off Between Electric Energy and Agriculture in the Four Corners Area," *Water Resources Research* 15(June 1979):529–538. For more discussion of the topic of water supply and regional economic growth see Maurice M. Kelso, William E. Martin, and Lawrence E. Mack, *Water Supplies and Economic Growth in an Arid Environment: An Arizona Case Study* (Tucson: University of Arizona Press, 1973).

11. It should be recognized that serious droughts lasting more than a decade appear to have occurred in past centuries. The "greenhouse effect" of CO_2 buildup reportedly could increase the likelihood of drought in the future.

12. These include significant opportunities for water conservation in agricultural, municipal, and industrial uses, as well as the agriculture/municipal conversion factor, which suggests that a little irrigation water can go a long way residentially.

13. See *Sporhase v. Nebraska*, 81 U.S. 613 (1982).

14. See U.S. District Court for the District of New Mexico, *The City of El Paso v. S. E. Reynolds*, Civ. No. 80-730 HB, January 17, 1983.

See also the opinion on New Mexico's change in law, U.S. District Court for the District of New Mexico, "Memorandum Opinion" in *The City of El Paso v. S. E. Reynolds,* August 3, 1984.

15. Equitable apportionment decrees have determined the share of an interstate stream to which a state is entitled. And compacts have protected some slower developing states from losing future claims to water from a stream as a result of faster development by another state on the stream system.

16. *Colorado v. New Mexico* II, 104 Supreme Court 2433 (1984).

17. For a discussion of the Galloway–San Diego proposal, see "Leaders Leery About Selling Water to San Diego," *Salt Lake Tribune,* Sept. 19, 1984.

18. See *Arizona v. California,* 373 U.S. 546 (1963).

19. See Elbert P. Tuttle, "Report of the Special Master, *Arizona v. California*" (Feb. 22, 1983).

20. Of five projected units in the CUP, two small units are complete and three are still under construction, as confirmed in telephone conversations with Ms. Theda Butt and Mrs. Kathy Loveless, Public Affairs Division, U.S. Bureau of Reclamation, Salt Lake City, Utah, October and November 1984.

21. Colorado's water development agenda for its western slope also still includes the Animas–La Plata project involving dam construction and irrigation works in southwestern Colorado. See, for example, "Saving Animas–La Plata in a Project-Wary Congress," editorial, *Denver Post,* June 24, 1984.

22. Arizona Department of Water Resources, Tucson Active Management Area, *Summary of the Proposed Management Plan* (Tucson, 1983).

23. For a full discussion of the competing viewpoints that underlay the 1980 Act, see Michael F. McNulty and Gary C. Woodard, "Arizona Water Issues: Contrasting Economic and Legal Perspectives," *Arizona Review* 32(Fall 1984):1–13.

24. *Report of the Select Committee on Water Marketing,* 49th Legislature, State of Montana, January 1985.

25. House Bill 680, 49th Legislature, State of Montana, July 1, 1985.

26. See William Martin, Helen Ingram, Nancy Laney, and Adrian Griffin, *Saving Water in a Desert City* (Washington, D.C.: Resources for the Future, 1984).

27. The New Mexico Public Service Commission recently granted the private company a 61.6 percent increase in rates (*Albuquerque Journal,* Jan. 22, 1985).

28. In a July 1986 report entitled "Western Water: Tuning the System," the Western Governors Association called for improvements in the efficiency of water use within the region and stated that "markets are preferable to regulation in moving water from one use to another." *Western Report,* July 18, 1986, No. 7.

3. THE COMMUNITY VALUE OF WATER
AND IMPLICATIONS FOR THE RURAL POOR

1. As examples, we may cite Robert Haveman, *The Economic Perform-ance of Public Investments: An Ex Post Evaluation of Water Resource Investments* (Baltimore, Md.: Johns Hopkins Press, 1972), 110–111: "The conclusions of this study are not encouraging. In a number of cases, inconsistencies were found between the ex ante evaluation procedures of the Corps of Engineers and those that would be derived from the basic efficiency model. In the case of navigation benefits, for example, the evaluation procedures applied by the agency have little, if any, relationship to an efficiency concept of benefits or any other benefit concept that has economic meaning. In the empirical case studies presented, ex post estimates of benefits often showed little relationship to their ex ante counterparts. On the basis of the few cases and the prior analysis presented here, one could conclude that there is a serious bias incorporated into agency ex ante evaluation procedures, resulting in persistent overstatement of expected benefits." Also, see H. S. Burness, Ronald G. Cummings, W. D. Gorman, and R. R. Lansford, "United States Reclamation Policy and Indian Water Rights," *Natural Resources Journal* 20(October 1980).

2. Many of the California water projects were constructed with state funding. Even small states such as New Mexico have constructed reservoirs such as Ute Dam in the eastern part of the state.

3. Colorado River Basin Project Act of 1968, 43 U.S.C., sec. 1511.

4. Edith Hamilton and Huntington Cairns, eds., *Plato: Collected Dialogues of Plato* (Westminster, Md.: Pantheon Books, 1961), 1,409.

5. Helen M. Ingram, Lawrence A. Scaff, and Leslie Silko, "Replacing Confusion with Equity: Alternatives for Water Policy in the Colorado River Basin," in *New Courses for the Colorado River, Major Issues for the Next Century*, ed. Gary D. Weatherford and F. Lee Brown (Albuquerque: University of New Mexico Press, 1986).

6. As quoted in Arthur Maas and Raymond Anderson, . . . *And the Desert Shall Rejoice: Conflict, Growth, and Justice in Arid Environments* (Cambridge: MIT Press, 1978), 2.

7. Kenneth Boulding, "The Implications of Improved Water Allocation Policy," in *Western Water Resources: Coming Problems and the Policy Alternatives: A Symposium*, sponsored by the Federal Reserve Bank of Kansas City, September 27–28, 1979 (Boulder, Colo.: Westview Press, 1980), 300.

8. Maurice Kelso, "The Water is Different Syndrome, or What is Wrong with the Water Industry?" (Paper presented to the American Water Resources Association, San Francisco, November 9, 1967).

9. Maass and Anderson, *And the Desert Shall Rejoice*, 5.

10. Helen Ingram and Stephen P. Mumme, "Public Perceptions of Water Issues in the Four Corners States as Indicated through a Survey of Regional Newspapers: A Preliminary Report" (Paper presented at

the Western Social Science Association's 25th Annual Conference, Albuquerque, N.M., April 27–30, 1983).

11. Meyer, *Water in the Hispanic Southwest*, 157.

12. Raymond Otis, *Little Valley* (London: Cresset Press, 1937; Albuquerque: University of New Mexico Press, 1980).

13. Ralph Moody, *Little Britches: Father and I Were Ranchers* (New York: W. W. Norton, 1950).

14. Florence Cranell Means, *The Rains Will Come* (Boston: Houghton Mifflin, 1954).

15. DuMars et al., *Pueblo Indian Water Rights*, 8.

16. Frank Waters, *The Man Who Killed the Deer* (New York: Farrar, Rinehart, 1941; New York: Pocket Books, 1973), 80.

17. Meyer, *Water in the Hispanic Southwest*, 151.

18. Ibid., 157.

19. Maass and Anderson, *And the Desert Shall Rejoice.*

20. Oliver LaFarge, *The Mother Ditch/La Acequia Madre* (Boston: Houghton Mifflin, 1954; Santa Fe, N.M.: Sunstone Press, 1983), 50.

21. Maass and Anderson, *And the Desert Shall Rejoice*, 27.

22. Ibid., 396.

23. Ibid., 370.

24. *Rio Grande Sun* (Espanola, New Mexico), Feb. 28, 1980.

25. E. Walter Coward, *Irrigation and Agricultural Development in Asia: Perspective from the Social Sciences* (Ithaca, N.Y.: Cornell University Press, 1980).

26. Sue Ellen Jacobs, "Top-down Planning: Analysis of Obstacles to Community Development in an Economically Poor Region of the Southwestern United States," *Human Organization* 37(no. 3, 1978):252.

27. "Water Battle in the Northwest: Coal, Uranium Firms Go after Rights," *Albuquerque Journal*, June 9, 1978, sec. E.

28. "Matheson Urges: 'Conserve Water Now,'" *Salt Lake Tribune*, Dec. 16, 1977.

29. Steve Winston, "A Slow Death on the Pecos," *Albuquerque Journal*, Feb. 25, 1980.

30. Robert C. Hunt and Eva Hunt, "Canal Irrigation and Local Social Organization," *Current Anthropology* 17(no. 3, 1976):394–397.

31. American Indian Lawyer Training Program Inc., *Indian Water Policy in a Changing Environment* (Oakland, Calif., 1982), 56.

32. Norris Hundley, jr., "The 'Winters' Decision and Indian Water Rights: A Mystery Reexamined," *Western Historical Quarterly* 13(January 1982):17–42.

33. Folk-Williams, *What Indian Water Means*, 38.

34. C. Vandemoer and R. Peters, "Indigenous Response to Water in an Arid Environment: A Papago Case Study" (Tucson: John Muir Institute for Environmental Studies, February 28, 1984), 44–45.

35. Hispanic field interviews.

36. Waters, *The Man Who Killed the Deer*, 24.

37. Helen M. Ingram, William E. Martin, and Nancy K. Laney, "A Willingness to Play: Analysis of Water Resources Development in Arizona," in *Water and Agriculture in the Western U.S.: Conservation, Reallocation, and Markets,* ed. Gary D. Weatherford (Boulder, Colo.: Westview Press, 1982).

38. Novesima Recopilacion, Libro III, Titulo 28, ley 31 (as quoted in Meyer, *Water in the Hispanic Southwest,* 21).

39. Editorial, *Albuquerque Journal,* Jan. 21, 1983.

40. See, for example, David Korten, "Community Organization and Rural Development: A Learning Process Approach," *Public Administration Review* 40(September/October 1980):480–510.

41. Steve Cox and Sheldon Annis, "Community Participation in Rural Water Supply, Grassroots Development," *Journal of the Inter-American Foundation* 6(no. 1, 1982).

42. For a more extended discussion of this point together with a review of some quantitative evidence, see B. Delworth Gardner, "The Untried Market Approach to Water Allocation," in *New Courses for the Colorado River,* ed. Gary D. Weatherford and F. Lee Brown (Albuquerque: University of New Mexico Press, 1986).

43. The terms of the compact make it practically very difficult to transfer a right across a compact accounting point, one of which occurs at Otowi Bridge just above Santa Fe. This point is discussed again in the Hispanic case study.

4. HISPANICS IN THE UPPER RIO GRANDE

1. Robert E. Clark, "Water Rights Problems in the Upper Rio Grande Watershed and Adjoining Areas," *Natural Resources Journal* 11(January 1971):48–68.

2. "The Spanish settlers brought to this continent a knowledge of irrigation institutions and practice acquired principally from the Moors and proceeded to adapt their irrigation experience to the new country. As a result Indian customs were modified but not extinguished, and out of the merging of the Spanish and Indian methods of public or community handling of irrigation affairs there developed the Spanish-American community acequia." Wells A. Hutchins, "The Community Acequia: Its Origins and Development," *Southwest Historical Quarterly* 31(no. 3, 1928):261.

3. "A Program of Support for Northern New Mexico Community Ditches" (A proposal prepared by the Home Education Livelihood Program—HELP, Albuquerque, N.M., 1978).

4. "Under the old Spanish law, waters were held by municipalities— pueblos or communes—as a common property for domestic use, irrigation, and other purposes, but while their utilization was free to all inhabitants of the town, it was governed by municipal rules, and regulated and controlled by the town officials. . . . The common proprietorship of water supplies, public construction of irrigation works,

and the administration of local irrigation affairs by separate communities were very important features of Moorish and Spanish institutions long before the discovery of the New World." Hutchins, "The Community Acequia," 264.

5. Marc Simmons, "Spanish Irrigation Practices in New Mexico," *New Mexico Historical Review* 97(January 1972):135–150.

6. Reservoir evaporation in the area occurs at Abiquiu, El Vado, and Heron dams; water in these three reservoirs is destined mainly for use in the middle and lower Rio Grande valley, outside the study area.

7. Much has been written about Hispanic culture in northern New Mexico. See, for example, Paul Hutsche and John Van Ness, *Canones: Values Crisis and Survival in a Northern New Mexico Village* (Albuquerque: University of New Mexico Press, 1981).

8. Tierra Amarilla was the setting in 1969 for a land dispute led by Reies Lopez Tijerina that erupted into fatal violence.

5. SAN JUAN–CHAMA, *AAMODT,* AND THE IMPORTANCE OF WATER TO TRADITIONAL HISPANICS

1. For exactness, Arizona's Upper Basin entitlement of fifty thousand acre-feet per year must be deducted before the 11.25 percent fraction is applied. Gilbert Bonem and F. Lee Brown, "Two Case Studies on the Relationship Between the Bureau of Reclamation and Other Governmental Agencies—Local, State, and Federal" (Corrales, N.M.: Center for Natural Resource Studies, January 31, 1983, mimeograph), 1–14.

2. Jack O. Horton, "Statement," in U.S. Congress, Senate Committee on Interior and Insular Affairs, *San Juan–Chama Project: Hearing before the Subcommittee on Energy Research and Water Resources,* 94th Cong., 1st sess., June 12, 1975, 7–14. This figure has been the subject of disagreement and occasional revision.

3. Bonem and Brown, *Two Case Studies,* 1–14.

4. Ibid., 1.

5. Ibid., 6.

6. U.S. Congress, Senate Committee on Interior and Insular Affairs, *Navajo Irrigation—San Juan–Chama Diversion: Hearings of the Subcommittee on Irrigation and Reclamation,* July 9–10, 1958, and March 15, 1961; U.S. Congress, House Committee on Interior and Insular Affairs, *San Juan–Chama Project and Navajo Indian Irrigation Project: Hearings of the Subcommittee on Irrigation and Reclamation,* May 20, 1960, and April 24–26 and June 1, 1961.

7. Senate Committee on Interior and Insular Affairs, *Navajo Irrigation,* July 9–10, 1958, 27.

8. John Nichols, "To Save a Dying Culture," *Race Relations Reporter,* 5(July 1974):20.

9. Ibid., 23.

10. Jacobs, "Top-Down Planning," 253.

11. Ibid.

12. Bonem and Brown, "Two Case Studies," 9–10.

13. Formally, *The State of New Mexico, ex.rel., S.E. Reynolds, State Engineer v. R. Lee Aamodt, et al. defendant and the United States of America, Pueblo of Nambe, Pueblo of Pojoaque, Pueblo of San Ildefonso, Pueblo of Tesuque.*

14. Actually, *Aamodt* is only one of several pending adjudication suits on the Rio Grande and its tributaries. The others are being held in abeyance, awaiting judicial resolution of some central issues common to all.

15. John Nichols, "New Water Problems Loom for Chicano Farmers," *Race Relations Reporter* 5(August 1974):6–7.

16. The term "practicably irrigable acreage" refers to the quantification standard for Indian water rights developed in the Special Master's Report, *Arizona v. California*, 373 U.S. 540 (1963). An extended discussion of this facet, and others, of the *Aamodt* litigation is contained in DuMars et al., *Pueblo Indian Water Rights.*

17. Stephen W. Terrell, "The Water Lawsuit's Bitter Taste," *Santa Fe Reporter*, Aug. 24, 1983.

18. Ibid.

19. Ibid.

20. Orlando Romero, "The *Aamodt* Case: An American Tragedy," *News and Review* (December 1983/January 1984).

21. Mary Frei, "Suit Pits Friend Against Friend," *Albuquerque Journal*, May 11, 1983.

22. Dan Herrera, "Water Suit a 'Defensive Battle' for Indians, Non-Indians Alike," *Santa Fe New Mexican*, March 18, 1980.

23. Ibid.

24. Ibid.

25. Dan Herrera, "Pueblo Council to Meet Today on Water Suit Fund Reduction," *Santa Fe New Mexican*, Oct. 25, 1979.

26. Anne Poore, "Senators Urge Fairness in Water Rights Suit," *Santa Fe New Mexican*, Jan. 7, 1980.

27. "Attorneys' Removal from Suit Denied," *Santa Fe New Mexican*, Feb. 2, 1980.

28. "Senators Request Legal Aid," *Santa Fe New Mexican*, Jan. 23, 1980.

29. "Leave *Aamodt* in Court," *Albuquerque Journal*, July 31, 1983, sec. B.

30. Helen Gaussoin, "Water Rights Settlement Possible," *Santa Fe New Mexican*, July 22, 1983; "Mediators Would Referee Water Rights," *Santa Fe New Mexican*, Aug. 5, 1983.

31. Lindy Johnson, "Water Group Encouraged by Officials," *Rio Grande Sun*, Aug. 11, 1983.

32. Mary Frei, "Pueblos Say No to *Aamodt* Talks," *Albuquerque Journal*, Aug. 25, 1983.

33. Mary Frei, "Domenici Seeks Funds for *Aamodt* Water Suit," *Albuquerque Journal*, Sept. 9, 1983.

34. The actual tabulation was 44 yes, 39 no, and 14 giving no firm answer.

6. ECONOMIC DEVELOPMENT AND HISPANIC PREFERENCES FOR WATER USE

1. See Marta Weigle, ed., *Hispanic Villages of Northern New Mexico*, a reprint of vol. 2 of the 1935 Tewa Basin Study (Santa Fe, N.M.: Lightning Tree Publishers, 1975).

2. J. T. Reid, *It Happened in Taos* (Albuquerque, N.M.: University of New Mexico Press, 1946).

3. John Burma and David Williams, "An Economic, Social, and Educational Survey of Rio Arriba and Taos Counties" (Report to Northern New Mexico College, El Rito, 1960).

4. Peter van Dresser, *Development on a Human Scale: Potentials for Ecologically Guided Growth in Northern New Mexico* (New York: Praeger Press, 1972).

5. Manuel Ferran, "Planning for Economic Development of Rural Northern New Mexico" (Ph.D. diss., University of Oklahoma, 1969).

6. North Central New Mexico Economic Development District, *Overall Economic Development Plan* (Santa Fe, N.M., 1970); and North Central New Mexico Economic Development District, *Regional Development Plan* (Santa Fe, N.M., 1977).

7. The summary volume of this study is Thomas Clevenger, William Capener, and John Canady, *Potential for Agriculture and Forestry Development in the Four Corners Region*, Agricultural Experiment Station Special Report 29 (Las Cruces: New Mexico State University, 1973). Individual reports include the following: Thomas Clevenger, John Canady, and Linda Demarest, *Feasibility of Expanded Vegetable Production and Canneries in the Four Corners Region* (1973); J'Wayne McArthur, Jay Andersen, and William Capener, *Feasibility of Establishing Alfalfa—Dehydrating Plants in the Four Corners Region* (1971); Albert Madsen, *Feasibility of Plywood Production in the Four Corners Region* (1972).

8. San Luis Valley Council of Governments, *San Luis Valley Labor Force Survey* (Alamosa, Colo., 1977).

9. San Luis Valley Regional Development and Planning Commission, *San Luis Valley Overall Economic Development Program* (Alamosa, Colo., 1980).

10. See Ben Mason and Tom Clevenger, "Achieving the Potential for Irrigated Agriculture in New Mexico," *New Mexico Business* 32(March 1979):3–13; and Tom Clevenger and Gene Ross, *Some Limitations to Agricultural Development in Northern New Mexico*, Department of Agricultural Economics Staff Report 36 (Las Cruces: New Mexico State University, September 1983).

11. Clair Reiniger Morris and associates, *Northern New Mexico: People and Water Resources Report* (Santa Fe, N.M.: Designwrights Collaborative, August 1983).

12. The tabulation in Table 6.1 of people who said that some water right sales were occurring may include some double counting. That is, some respondents may be referring to the same water right sale or sales. The extent of this double counting is unknown, as is the actual number of water right sales during the last five years.

13. Whether respondents were citing prices for an acre-foot of diversion rights or consumptive use rights was unclear. Typically, consumptive use is 50–60 percent of diversions, and this difference is insufficient to account for the large discrepancy in prices.

14. We would like to thank Nathaniel Wollman of the University of New Mexico for helping us develop this recreational alternative.

15. Under the terms of the Rio Grande Compact, Colorado has been in deficit to New Mexico and Texas for a number of years. Consequently, natural shortfalls in water availability in those counties have been made worse by institutional rules.

7. POSSIBILITIES FOR UPPER RIO GRANDE AGRICULTURE

1. Tom Clevenger and Paula Carpenter, *Irrigated Acreage in New Mexico and Estimate Crop Values by County, 1980*, Agricultural Experiment Station Research Report 498 (Las Cruces: New Mexico State University, 1983).

2. See particularly Ferran, *Planning for Economic Development;* North Central New Mexico Economic Development District, *Regional Development Plan;* and Thomas Clevenger and David Kraenzels, *A History of Vegetable Crops in New Mexico*, Agricultural Experiment Station Bulletin 624 (Las Cruces: New Mexico State University, August 1974).

3. An initial shift of perhaps 3,500 acres to vegetables and fruits, out of 78,000 irrigated acres in the three northern New Mexico counties, over a three- to six-year period might be feasible. This transition could be followed by a further shift as the practicality of this cropping pattern became more established and accepted.

4. Tom Clevenger, "Some Limitations to Agricultural Development in Northern New Mexico" (New Mexico State University, Las Cruces, August 1983).

5. See, for example, Nancie L. Gonzales, *The Spanish-Americans of New Mexico: A Heritage of Pride* (Albuquerque: University of New Mexico Press, 1969).

6. Our description of the Ganados del Valle program relies on a paper by Maria Varela, "Ganados del Valle: A Rural Self Reliance Venture," presented in 1985 at Utah State University, and Jeanne P. Fleming, "Ganados del Valle, A Venture in Self-Sufficiency," *New Mexico*

Magazine, September 1985. Discussions with Maria Varela of Ganados del Valle were also important to the description of the program.

8. WATER AND OPPORTUNITY IN THE UPPER RIO GRANDE

1. New Mexico state water official, private conversation with authors.
2. *Ensenada Land & Water Association et al. v. Howard M. Sleeper et al. and Steve Reynolds, New Mexico State Engineer,* No. RA-84-53 (C).
3. Judge Art Encinias, letter to counsel in Ensenada Ditch case, April 16, 1985.
4. House Bill 192, 1985 New Mexico state legislature.

9. THE TOHONO O'ODHAM NATION

1. H. Manuel, J. Ramon, and B. Fontana, "Alternative Economic Development Policies for Indian Communities. Dressing for the Window: Papago Indians and Economic Development" (Report prepared for the Economic Development Administration, U.S. Department of Commerce, July 1974), 36a, 41–43; reprinted in S. Stanley, ed., *American Indian Economic Development* (Paris: Mouton, 1978).
2. U.S. Census (1980). Adapted from Bureau of Applied Research in Anthropology, "Socio-Cultural Impact Assessment of the San Xavier Planned Community" (Tucson: University of Arizona, 1984).
3. Frank S. Crosswhite, "The Annual Saguaro Harvest and Crop Cycle of the Papago, with Reference to Ecology and Symbolism," *Desert Plants* 2(no. 1, 1980).
4. Ruth M. Underhill, *Papago Indian Religion* (New York: Columbia University Press, 1946).
5. Ibid., 135.
6. Crosswhite, "Annual Saguaro Harvest," 56.
7. Ibid.
8. Bernard L. Fontana, "Pima and Papago: Introduction," in *Handbook of North American Indians,* vol. 10, *Southwest,* ed. Alfonso Ortiz (Washington, D.C.: Smithsonian Institution, 1983), 125–136.
9. Robert A. Hackenberg, "Pima and Papago Ecological Adaptations," in *Handbook of North American Indians,* vol. 10, *Southwest,* ed. Alfonso Ortiz (Washington, D.C.: Smithsonian Institution, 1983), 161–177.
10. Ronald U. Cooke and Richard W. Reeves, *Arroyos and Environmental Change in the American South-West* (London and New York: Oxford Clarendon Press, 1976).
11. Henry F. Dobyns, *From Fire to Flood: Historic Human Destruction of Sonoran Desert Riverine Oases* (Socorro, N.M.: Ballena Press, 1981).

10. TOHONO O'ODHAM PARTICIPATION IN WATER RESOURCE DEVELOPMENT: CONSTRAINTS AND OPPORTUNITIES

1. Coward, *Irrigation and Agricultural Development.*

2. American Indian Policy Review Commission (AIPRC), *Final Report,* vol. 1 (Washington, D.C.: U.S. Government Printing Office, 1977), 128.

3. U.S. Congress, Senate Committee on Indian Affairs, *Survey of Conditions of the Indians in the United States: Hearings before Subcommittee,* 71st Cong., 3d sess., part 17 (Washington, D.C.: U.S. Government Printing Office, 1931), 8384.

4. Ibid., 8371.

5. "Papago Indians Growing Cotton," *Tucson Citizen,* Oct. 13, 1929.

6. Ibid.

7. Ibid.

8. "Schools and Water Asked for Papagos," *Tucson Citizen,* April 21, 1931.

9. "Papago Trouble, Need of Water, Senators Told," *Arizona Daily Star,* April 21, 1931.

10. Robert A. Hackenberg, "Colorado River Basin Development and Its Potential Impact on Tribal Life, *Human Organization* 35(Fall 1976):303–311.

11. "Hope Seen for 'Graveyard' Papago Indian Reservations," *Tucson Citizen,* Oct. 7, 1970.

12. "Papagos Ask $500,000 to Save Cattle Decimated by Drought," *Tucson Citizen,* July 19, 1969.

13. "Uncle Sam Disappoints Papagos," *Phoenix Gazette,* July 19, 1969.

14. J. Smith, "Tat Momolikot Dam—A Second Papago Disaster," *Tucson Citizen,* Aug. 26, 1977, sec. A.

15. Ibid.

16. Ibid.

17. Ibid.

18. Ibid.

19. Ibid.

20. C. Sonnichsen, *Tucson—The Life and Times of an American City* (Norman: University of Oklahoma Press, 1982), 110.

21. T. W. Anderson, *Electrical Analog Analysis of the Hydrologic System, Tucson Basin, Southeastern Arizona,* U.S. Geological Survey, Water Supply Paper 1939-6, U.S. Department of Interior (Washington, D.C.: U.S. Government Printing Office, 1972), C12.

22. Senate Committee on Indian Affairs, *Survey of Conditions,* 8,382.

23. Ibid.

24. Ibid., 8,383.

25. Ibid., 8,348.

26. Ibid., 8,358.

27. Ibid., 8,367.

28. P. Blaine, Sr., and M. S. Adams, *Papagos and Politics* (Tucson: Arizona Historical Society, 1981), 67.

29. Graham Taylor, *The New Deal and American Indian Tribalism* (Lincoln: University of Nebraska Press, 1980), 78.

30. A. Joseph, J. Chesky, and R. Spicer, *The Desert People* (Chicago: University of Chicago Press, 1949), 104.

31. Manuel, Ramon, and Fontana, "Alternative Economic Development Policies," 48.

32. Taylor, *New Deal and Tribalism*, 80.

33. Robert Bee, *The Politics of American Indian Policy* (Cambridge, Mass.: Schenkman Publishing Company, 1982).

34. Ibid., 33.

35. Vandemoer and Peters, "Indigenous Response to Water," 2.

36. Manuel, Ramon, and Fontana, "Alternative Economic Development Policies," 49.

37. Ibid.

38. Ibid., 50.

39. "Some Points to Consider about the Constitution," *Papago Runner*, Jan. 16, 1986, 8.

40. Vandemoer and Peters, "Indigenous Response to Water," 9.

41. *Winters v. United States*, 207 U.S. 564 (1908).

42. AIPRC, *Final Report*, 329.

43. *Arizona v. California*, 373 U.S. 546 (1963).

44. A. Shrago, "Emerging Indian Water Rights: An Analysis of Recent Judicial and Legislative Developments," *Rocky Mountain Mineral Law Institute* 26(1980):1,116.

45. *Cappaert v. United States*, 426 U.S. 128 (1976).

46. Fradkin, *A River No More*.

11. THE TOHONO O'ODHAM TAKE INITIATIVE

1. Ben MacNitt, "Water Claim: Settle or Sue?" *Tucson Citizen*, Feb. 6, 1980, sec. C.

2. Ibid.

3. Editorial, *Arizona Daily Star*, June 14, 1982, sec. A.

4. Ernie Heltsley, "Water Rights Are Battlefield in '1980 Indian War,'" *Arizona Daily Star*, Nov. 30, 1980, sec. B.

5. Complaint, *United States v. City of Tucson*, CIV 75-39 TUC (D. Arizona).

6. Heltsley, "Water Rights."

7. Ibid.

8. Ibid.

9. William Strickland, Tohono O'odham tribal attorney, Arizona Groundwater Commission Meeting, January 25, 1978.

10. Steve Meissner, "Veto of Udall's Water Rights Bill Is More of the Same for Papagos," *Arizona Daily Star*, June 6, 1982, sec. A.

11. Michael Thuss, "Negotiating the Water Future of Pima County, Arizona" (Report for U.S. Army Corps of Engineers, Los Angeles District, Tucson Urban Study, 1977), 3.

12. U.S. Army Corps of Engineers, Los Angeles District, Tucson Urban Study, "Eastern Pima County Water Resources Plan: A Preliminary Analysis" (Report prepared for the Water Resources Coordinating Committee, June 26, 1979).

13. Ibid., 1.

14. Ibid.

15. Cecil Andrus, secretary of interior, speech at Central Arizona Project Meeting, Phoenix, Arizona (October 5, 1979), 12.

16. Ibid., 4.

17. Ibid., 7.

18. "A Southern Arizona Lament," editorial, *Arizona Daily Star*, June 14, 1981, sec. C.

19. Anne Hyde, "Now or Never, Udall Warns on CAP Questions," *Arizona Daily Star*, March 4, 1981, sec. B.

20. Ibid.

21. *Congressional Record*, 97th Cong., 2d sess., House 673-74, 681-82, March 4, 1982.

22. U.S. Congress, Senate Select Committee on Interior Affairs, *Hearing on S. 2114, H.R. 5118*, 97th Cong., 2d sess., 1982, 66.

23. "In Reservation Water Issue the Standard Is Change," *Papago Runner*, July 7, 1980.

24. Ibid.

25. Carol Pateman, *Participation and Democratic Theory* (Cambridge: Cambridge University Press, 1970), 71.

26. WRCC, meeting minutes, October 7, 1981.

27. "Senate's Water Bill Expected to Move Following Hearing," *Papago Runner*, April 2, 1982.

28. Senate Select Committee on Interior Affairs, *Hearing on S. 2114*, 95.

29. Mark Ulmer, former Tohono O'odham legal services attorney, personal interview by Catherine Vandemoer and Ramona Peters, July 28, 1983.

30. *Congressional Quarterly Almanac* (1982):24E.

31. Ibid.

32. Anne Hoy, "Udall Ready to Plunge into New Negotiations on Papago Water Fight," *Arizona Daily Star*, June 5, 1982, sec. A.

33. Steve Meissner, "Indian Water Negotiators Picked, Goldwater Says," *Arizona Daily Star*, July 14, 1982, sec. B.

34. Steve Meissner, "Water Talks Hit Sticky Point," *Arizona Daily Star*, Aug. 6, 1982, sec. B.

35. Ibid.

36. Ibid.

37. Ibid.

38. U.S. Congress, Senate Committee of Conference, *Conference*

Report to S. 1409, S. Rept. 97-568, Title III (Washington, D.C.: U.S. Government Printing Office, 1982), 49.

12. SAWRSA AND TOHONO O'ODHAM PREFERENCES

1. The Southern Arizona Water Rights Settlement Act (SAWRSA), 1983 [P.L. 97-293, sec. 307(c)(1)].
2. Ibid., sec. 304(c)(2).
3. Ibid., sec. 302(a).
4. Nancy Laney, "Transferability Under the Papago Water Rights Settlement," *Arizona Law Review* 26(1984):421.
5. SAWRSA, sec. 303(3).
6. Ibid., sec. 313(f).
7. Korten, "Community Organization and Rural Development."
8. Vandemoer and Peters, "Indigenous Responses to Water."
9. Bureau of Applied Research in Anthropology (BARA), "Socio-Cultural Impact Assessment of the San Xavier Planned Community, Papago Indian Reservation, Pima County, Arizona" (Tucson: University of Arizona, 1984), Appendix B.

13. TOHONO O'ODHAM OPPORTUNITIES FOR RESOURCE USE

1. Manuel, Ramon, and Fontana, "Alternative Economic Development Policies." See also Rolf W. Bauer, "The Papago Cattle Economy: Implications for Economic and Community Development in Arid Lands," in *Food, Fiber and the Arid Lands*, ed. W. G. McGinnies, Bram J. Goldman, and Patricia Paylore (Tucson: University of Arizona Press, 1971); and Henry F. Dobyns, "Blunders with *Bolsas*," *Human Organization* 31(no. 2, 1951):25–32.
2. Dobyns, "Blunders with *Bolsas*."
3. Ibid., 31.
4. Manuel, Ramon, and Fontana, "Alternative Economic Development Policies."
5. *Papago Tribal Constitution and By-Laws*, Article XVIII, 1984 Revisions.
6. Reid Peyton Chambers and Monroe E. Price, "Regulating Sovereignty: Secretarial Discretion and the Leasing of Indian Lands," *Stanford Law Review* 26(1974):1,061–1,096. See also Dennis R. Ickes, "Tribal Economic Independence: The Means to Achieve True Tribal Self-Determination," *South Dakota Law Review* 26(1981):494.
7. MacNitt, "Water Claim."
8. Ibid.
9. Deborah Sliz, counsel, Subcommittee on Energy and Environment, Committee on Interior and Insular Affairs, U.S. House of Representatives. Interview with Jean Florman, Tom McGuire, and Mary Wallace, September 11, 1983, 10.
10. SAWRSA, sec. 306(c).

11. Laney, "Papago Water Rights Settlement," 437.

12. Ibid., 440.

13. Ibid., 435.

14. ASARCO, Inc., Lease with Tohono O'odham Tribe, negotiated by Ed Berger, Tohono O'odham tribal attorney, September 7, 1972, sec. 1.

15. SAWRSA, sec. 304(e)(2).

16. Laney, "Papago Water Rights Settlement," 437.

17. SAWRSA, sec. 304(e)(1)(A).

18. Bobbie Jo Buel, "Some Big Water Users Wary of CAP," *Arizona Daily Star*, March 16, 1984, sec. A.

19. Laney, "Papago Water Rights Settlement," 437.

20. Ibid., 438.

21. SAWRSA, sec. 305(b)(1).

22. Ibid., sec. 306(c)(2).

23. Laney, "Papago Water Rights Settlement," 439.

24. Ibid., 440.

25. Buel, "Big Water Users."

26. Lester Snow, director, Tucson Active Management Area, telephone interview, August 22, 1984.

27. R. Williams, "Policy Statement Overview: Reagan's Initiatives Lead to More Questions Than Answers," *Indian Truth* (no. 250, 1983):17.

28. E. Williams, "Too Little Land, Too Many Heirs—the Indian Heirship Land Problem," *Washington Law Review* 45(1971):712.

29. T. Davis, "Developer Rethinking Papago Plan," *Tucson Citizen*, May 3, 1985, sec. D.

30. E. Heltsley, "Papago Council Tells Developer to Start Over," *Arizona Daily Star*, May 3, 1985, sec. B.

31. Ibid.

32. J. DeWitt, "Papago Voters Shut Out Development Backers," *Arizona Daily Star*, May 29, 1985, sec. B.

33. Davis, "Developer Rethinking Plan."

14. STRATEGIES FOR THE FUTURE

1. Gary P. Nabhan, *The Desert Smells Like Rain* (San Francisco: North Point Press, 1982), 8.

2. Ibid., 32.

3. Ibid., 48.

4. Ibid., 42.

5. Vandemoer and Peters, "Indigenous Response to Water."

6. Ibid.

7. MacNitt, "Water Claim."

8. Tony Davis, "Papagos Veto Large Project: Californian Planned 18,000-Acre Development," *Tucson Citizen*, May 2, 1985, sec. A.

9. Nabhan, *Desert Smells Like Rain;* Bernard L. Fontana, "Development Proposal for the San Xavier Indian Reservation: A Clash in Value Systems," *Arid Lands Newsletter* (no. 20, 1984); Bernard L. Fontana, "Pima and Papago: Introduction," in *Handbook of North American Indians,* vol. 10, *Southwest,* ed. Alfonso Ortiz (Washington, D.C.: Smithsonian Institution, 1983), 125–136; Bernard L. Fontana, "History of the Papago," in *Handbook of North American Indians,* vol. 10, *Southwest,* ed. Alfonso Ortiz (Washington, D.C.: Smithsonian Institution, 1983), 137–148; Bernard L. Fontana, *Of Earth and Little Rain: The Papago Indians* (Flagstaff, Ariz.: Northland Press, 1981); Bernard L. Fontana, "A History of the Legal Status of Land and of Land Use on the San Xavier Indian Reservation, Arizona" (Arizona State Museum, Tucson, Ariz.); Charles Bowden, *Killing the Hidden Waters* (Austin: University of Texas Press, 1977).

10. There is, for example, an exhibit on the Gila River Reservation funded by the Arizona Humanities Council.

11. Davis, "Papagos Veto Large Project."

16. WATER: OPPORTUNITY AND CHALLENGE

1. B. Delworth Gardner, "Institutional Impediments to Efficient Water Allocation," *Policy Studies Review* 5(November 1985):353–363; also Gardner, "Untried Market Approach."

2. Terry Anderson, *Water Crisis: Ending the Policy Drought* (Baltimore, Md.: Johns Hopkins University Press, 1983).

3. The Hon. Art Encinias, *In the Matter of Howard Sleeper, et al.,* Rio Arriba County Case No. RA 84-53(C).

4. John Gaventa, *Power and Powerlessness: Quiescence and Rebellion in an Appalachian Valley* (Urbana: University of Illinois Press, 1980).

5. Coward, *Irrigation and Agricultural Development.*

6. House Bill 192, enacted in the 1985 legislative session.

7. The Ensenada Ditch case.

INDEX